THE HANDY GUIDE TO

NEW TESTAMENT GREEK

Grammar, Syntax, and
Diagramming

Douglas S. Huffman

The Handy Guide to New Testament Greek: Grammar, Syntax, and Diagramming

© 2012 by Douglas S. Huffman

Published by Kregel Publications, a division of Kregel Inc., 2450 Oak Industrial Dr. NE, Grand Rapids, MI 49505.

Library of Congress Cataloging-in-Publication Data

Huffman, Douglas S.
   The handy guide to New Testament Greek : grammar, syntax, and diagramming / Douglas S. Huffman.
      p. cm.
   Includes bibliographical references (pp. 107-112).
  1. Greek language, Biblical—Grammar—Problems, exercises, etc. 2. Greek language, Biblical—Grammar—Outlines, syllabi, etc. 3. Bible. N.T.—Language, style—Problems, exercises, etc. 4. Bible. N.T.—Language, style—Outlines, syllabi, etc. I. Title.
   PA817.H84 2010
   487'.4—dc22   2010027963

The Greek font SymbolMetU is available from www.linguistsoftware.com/lgku. htm, +1-425-775-1130.

ISBN 978-0-8254-2743-5

Printed in the United States of America

20 21 22 23 24 25 26 / 6 5 4 3

CONTENTS

INTRODUCTION

In a book like this one, the answers to a few basic questions are important: for *whom* the book was written, *what* the book is (and is not), *why* the book was written, *where* it fits into the larger study of its discipline, *how* it might best be used, and *when* the reader would find it useful.

Who: This volume is intended for second-year Greek students (and beyond), pastors, teachers, and preachers. Constant NT Greek users (addicts!) might not need it, but would-be experts should find it useful.

What: When it comes to the study of NT Greek, this book is more of a collection of helpful tools than explanatory tales. It will not replace grammar and syntax textbooks, but it will supplement them nicely. In addition to reviewing grammar and syntax, this volume teaches phrase diagramming as a tool to discover sermon and lesson outlines quickly in the Greek text.

Why: This volume has been created because one year of Greek is dangerous; the language needs review and further study to become truly usable in the study of the Greek NT. The book is designed to be less cumbersome and more readily accessible than carrying around larger grammar and syntax textbooks.

Where: Since it presumes some of the basics of NT Greek, this book fits into the Greek learning sequence after a full year of elementary Greek has been mastered and then during and beyond the second year of NT Greek studies.

How: Intended as a useful tool and ready reference for the continued study of the Greek NT, even the physical dimensions of this volume are set at handbook size so as to fit with the Greek NT—either the United Bible Societies' 4th edition (the burgundy UBS[4]) or the Nestle-Aland 28th edition (the blue NA[28]).

When: If kept on hand with the Greek NT, this volume could be in constant use, assisting in the preparation of NT lessons and sermons.

I would like to acknowledge here the many helpful resources that have been mine over the years of my study of New Testament Greek. These have included my Greek professors, my former colleagues at Northwestern College, particularly the ancient and classical languages professors who have offered helpful input, and my several generations of Greek students (both at Trinity Evangelical Divinity School and at

Northwestern College) who have endured my practicing on them over the years. I owe a special debt of thanks to my first group of NT Greek students at Biola University, especially those who helped proofread this little volume, and to my friend Jay E. Smith (professor of New Testament Studies at Dallas Theological Seminary) who did the same. With large gratitude, I dedicate this small volume to my Greek instructors (in the order of my taking their Greek courses): Professors Wayne Bennedict (Elementary Greek), Walter Dunnett (Intermediate Greek), Walter Elwell (Greek Exegesis), and D. A. Carson (Advanced Greek Grammar). *Soli Deo gloria.*

PART I

GREEK GRAMMAR REMINDERS
With Enough English to Be Manageable

ALPHABET: Greek Letters Look Like This

GREEK LETTERS			ENGLISH EQUIVALENTS	
Alpha	A	α	a	as in father
Beta	B	β	b	as in brother
Gamma	Γ	γ	g	as in good
Delta	Δ	δ	d	as in dog
Epsilon	E	ε	e	as in elephant
Zeta	Z	ζ	z	as in maze
Eta	H	η	ē	as in obey
Theta	Θ	θ	th	as in thin
Iota	I	ι	i	as in intrigue
Kappa	K	κ	k	as in kid
Lamda	Λ	λ	l	as in lid
Mu	M	μ	m	as in mom
Nu	N	ν	n	as in nun
Xi	Ξ	ξ	x	as in axiom
Omicron	O	o	o	as in hot
Pi	Π	π	p	as in pot
Rho	P	ρ	r	as in rot
Sigma	Σ	σ, ς	s	as in sisters

Tau	T	τ	t	as in talk
Upsilon	Υ	υ	u/y	as in Lüdwig
Phi	Φ	φ	ph	as in phone
Chi	X	χ	ch	as in Bach
Psi	Ψ	ψ	ps	as in lips
Omega	Ω	ω	ō	as in go

BREATHING MARKS: "Ha" or "Ah"

On words beginning with a vowel (or ρ), a rough breathing mark (') indicates pronouncing an H sound in front of the vowel: ἁγιάζω is pronounced *ha-gi-A-dzō*. A smooth breathing mark (') indicates no H sound: ἀγαπάω is pronounced *a-ga-PA–ō*.

ACCENTS: Three Is the Key

There are three kinds of accents: acute (´), circumflex (ˆ), and grave (`) and they can appear only on a Greek word's last three syllables, which have names. In the three-syllable word ἄνθρωπος (pronounced *AN-thrō-pos*), the accent falls on the antepenult syllable.

ἄν   –   θρω   –   πος
Antepenult   –   Penult   –   Ultima

Accent /Syllable	Antepenult	Penult	Ultima
Acute (´) On any of the syllables.	Only when Ultima has a short vowel.		Changes to a grave if followed by another word.
Circumflex (ˆ) Only on long vowels in last two syllables.	NEVER	Only when Ultima has a short vowel.	
Grave (`) Only on the Ultima.	NEVER	NEVER	Changes to acute if the last syllable in a sentence.
This chart is modified from Walter Mueller, *Grammatical Aids for Students of New Testament Greek* (Grand Rapids: Eerdmans, 1972), 13.			

As nouns are declined (i.e., spelled in their various case forms), they tend to retain their accents on the same syllable (a.k.a. *consistent accent*). In the conjugation of verbs, however, their accents tend to recede as far toward the beginning of the word as the rules will allow (a.k.a. *recessive accent*).

Proclitics (e.g., εἰ, εἰς, ἐκ, ἐν, ὁ, ἡ, τό, οὐ, ὡς, etc.) are words that regularly lose their accents to the next word, and *enclitics* (e.g., εἰμί, μοῦ, μοί, μέ, ποτέ, σοῦ, σοί, σέ, etc.) are words that regularly lose their accents to the previous word (e.g., οὗτός ἐστιν ὁ υἱός μου ὁ ἀγαπητός, ἀκούετε αὐτοῦ in Mark 9:7).

NOUNS: Case Endings Are Function Flags

INTRODUCTION: GREEK NOUN BASICS

While English uses word order, Greek nouns alter their end spellings to identify their use in the sentence. Thus, the case endings flag the function of the noun in the sentence.

Nominative: The naming case; typically *nominates* the subject.

Genitive: The most flexible "of" case; typically *generates* some description of the preceding noun.

Dative: The case of personal interest; as in *dating*, typically names "to/for" whom an action is done.

Accusative: Identifies the extent or limits of the verb's action; makes *accusation* about what the subject did.

Vocative: The calling case; *vocalizes* who is being addressed (the nominative case spelling is often used instead).

Three groupings of nouns (called "declensions") follow different case spelling patterns and each has subgroupings with gender labels: masculine, feminine, and neuter.

BASIC CASE ENDINGS BY DECLENSION (see variations in subsequent tables)						
		First		**Second**		**Third**
		Fem.	Masc.	Masc.	Neu.	M. / F.	Neu.
SINGULAR	Nom.	-α / -η	-ας /-ης	-ος	-ον	various	–
	Gen.	-ας /-ης	-ου	-ου	-ου	-(τ)ος	-(τ)ος
	Dat.	-α / -η	-α / -η	-ῳ	-ῳ	-(τ)ι	-(τ)ι
	Acc.	-αν/-ην	-αν/-ην	-ον	-ον	-α	–
		First		**Second**		**Third**
		Fem.	Masc.	Masc.	Neu.	M./F.	Neu.
PLURAL	Nom.	-αι	-αι	-οι	-α	-(τ)ες	-(τ)α
	Gen.	-ων	-ων	-ων	-ων	-(τ)ων	-(τ)ων
	Dat.	-αις	-αις	-οις	-οις	-σι(ν)	-σι(ν)
	Acc.	-ας	-ας	-ους	-α	-(τ)ας	-(τ)α

First Declension: α DECLENSION

1. The various types within this declension differ primarily between words whose stems end in ε, ι, or ρ and those whose don't. (Thus, we might nickname some of these the "Old MacDonald" nouns—you know, "e, i, e, i, rho"!).

2. The plural endings are consistently the same for all types.

3. Singular masculine forms have -ς in the nominative and -ου in the genitive; e.g., δεσπότης ("master"), κριτής ("judge"), μαθητής, ("disciple"), προφήτης ("prophet").

4. Accents are consistent and follow the lexical form (nominative) unless the accent rules demand a change.

FIRST DECLENSION: α Declension Nouns

		Long -α Type	Short -α Type	Short -α Type
		Fem.: ε, ι, ρ	Fem.: ε, ι, ρ	Fem.: non- ε, ι, ρ
SINGULAR	Nom.	χώρα	ἀλήθεια	δόξα
	Gen.	χώρας	ἀληθείας	δόξης
	Dat.	χώρᾳ	ἀληθείᾳ	δόξῃ
	Acc.	χώραν	ἀλήθειαν	δόξαν
PLURAL	Nom.	χῶραι	ἀλήθειαι	δόξαι
	Gen.	χωρῶν	ἀληθειῶν	δοξῶν
	Dat.	χώραις	ἀληθείαις	δόξαις
	Acc.	χώρας	ἀληθείας	δόξας
		-η Type	-ας Type	-ης Type
		Fem.: non- ε, ι, ρ	Masc.: ε, ι, ρ	Masc.: non- ε, ι, ρ
SINGULAR	Nom.	σκηνή	νεανίας	μαθητής
	Gen.	σκηνῆς	νεανίου	μαθητοῦ
	Dat.	σκηνῇ	νεανίᾳ	μαθητῇ
	Acc.	σκηνήν	νεανίαν	μαθητήν
PLURAL	Nom.	σκηναί	νεανίαι	μαθηταί
	Gen.	σκηνῶν	νεανιῶν	μαθητῶν
	Dat.	σκηναῖς	νεανίαις	μαθηταῖς
	Acc.	σκηνάς	νεανίας	μαθητάς

Second Declension: o declension

1. This declension has fewer quirks than the first declension.

2. The genitive and dative endings (singular and plural) are consistently the same in both types of o-declension nouns.

3. In the neuter paradigm, the nominative and accusative spellings are the same in the singular and again are the same in the plural.

4. A few feminine words follow the masculine paradigm; e.g., ἄβυσσος ("abyss"), ἄμπελος ("vine"), βίβλος ("book"), νῆσος ("island"), ὁδός ("way, road"), ῥάβδος ("rod, staff").

5. Accents are consistent and follow the lexical form (nominative) unless the accent rules demand a change. If accented on the ultima in genitive or dative (singular or plural), the circumflex is used.

		-ος Type Masc.	-ον Type Neu.
SINGULAR	Nom.	λόγος	δῶρον
	Gen.	λόγου	δώρου
	Dat.	λόγῳ	δώρῳ
	Acc.	λόγον	δῶρον
PLURAL	Nom.	λόγοι	δῶρα
	Gen.	λόγων	δώρων
	Dat.	λόγοις	δώροις
	Acc.	λόγους	δῶρα

SECOND DECLENSION: o Declension Nouns

THIRD DECLENSION: CONSONANT DECLENSION

1. This declension has more quirks than the other two combined.

2. The final letter in the noun stem (usually a consonant) is the basis for distinguishing the declension's various types.

3. Some consonants fall into particular groups. Liquid consonants include λ, μ, ν, and ρ. Mute consonants include π, β, φ (labials), τ, δ, θ (dentals), and κ, γ, χ (palatals /velars).

4. The noun stem is typically visible in the genitive singular form but not the nominative singular (i.e., lexical) form.

5. Forming the case endings of third declension nouns often appeals to the rules for contraction (see chart below).

6. Accents are consistent and follow the lexical form unless the stem is monosyllabic, in which case all the genitive and dative case forms will be accented on the ultima.

GENERAL CONTRACTION RULES			
CONSONANTAL "SQUARE OF STOPS"	+ σ	+ κ	+ θ
Labials: π, β, φ	ψ	φ	φθ
Palatals (a.k.a. Velars): κ, γ, χ	ξ	χ	χθ
Dentals: τ, δ, θ *	σ	κ	σθ

* ν tends to contract like a dental and simply drop out, particularly when with τ:
αντ + σι = ασι / εντ + σι = εισι / οντ + σι = ουσι

VOWEL COMBINATIONS (most common: ει and ου)												
+	α	ε	η	ι	ο	υ	ω	αι	ει	η	οι	ου
α	α	α	α	αι	ω	αυ	ω	ᾳ	ᾳ*	ᾳ	ῳ	ω
ε	η	ει	η	ει	ου	ευ	ω	ῃ	ει	η	οι	ου
ο	ω	ου	ω†	οι	ου	ου	ω	ῳ	οι§	οι	οι	ου

* α and §ου in some words with -ειν infinitives; †ω in subjunctive of μι verbs.

THIRD DECLENSION: Consonant Declension Nouns

		Mute Type			Liquid Type	
		Regular			Regular	Syncopated
		Masc.	Fem.	Neu.	M./F.	M./F.
Stem		ἀρχοντ–	σαρκ–	ὀνοματ–	χείρ–	πατερ–
SINGULAR	Nom.	ἄρχων	σάρξ	ὄνομα	χείρ	πατήρ
	Gen.	ἄρχοντος	σαρκός	ὀνόματος	χειρός	πατρός
	Dat.	ἄρχοντι	σαρκί	ὀνόματι	χειρί	πατρί
	Acc.	ἄρχοντα	σάρκα	ὄνομα	χεῖρα	πατέρα
PLURAL	Nom.	ἄρχοντες	σάρκες	ὀνόματα	χεῖρες	πατέρες
	Gen.	ἀρχόντων	σαρκῶν	ὀνομάτων	χειρῶν	πατέρων
	Dat.	ἄρχουσι(ν)	σαρξί(ν)	ὀνόμασι(ν)	χερσί(ν)	πατράσι(ν)
	Acc.	ἄρχοντας	σάρκας	ὀνόματα	χεῖρας	πατέρας

Notes: Words can't end in τ so it drops off in sg. nom./acc. of neu. –ματ- nouns and from the end of –ντ- nouns in sg. nom. Liquid types have lengthened stem vowel in sg. nom., and a short stem vowel drops out in dats. and sg. gen.

		-ς Types		Vowel Types		
		-α·ς	-ε·ς	-ι Stem	-υ Stem	Diphthong
		Neu.	Neu.	Fem.	Masc.	Masc.
Stem		κρεα·ς	γενε·ς	πολι–	ἰχθυ–	βασιλευ–
SINGULAR	Nom.	κρέας	γένος	πόλις	ἰχθύς	βασιλεύς
	Gen.	κρέως	γένους	πόλεως	ἰχθύος	βασιλέως
	Dat.	κρέαι	γένει	πόλει	ἰχθύι	βασιλεῖ
	Acc.	κρέας	γένος	πόλιν	ἰχθύν	βασιλέα
PLURAL	Nom.	κρέα	γένη	πόλεις	ἰχθύες	βασιλεῖς
	Gen.	κρεῶν	γενῶν	πόλεων	ἰχθύων	βασιλέων
	Dat.	κρέασι(ν)	γένεσι(ν)	πόλεσι(ν)	ἰχθύσι(ν)	βασιλεῦσι(ν)
	Acc.	κρέα	γένη	πόλεις	ἰχθύας	βασιλεῖς

Notes: ς stays in sg. nom./acc., but –ες nouns have –ος in sg. nom./acc. ι stays only in sg. nom./acc. and is ε elsewhere in -ι nouns. υ remains for –υ nouns, but in –ευ nouns drops before endings with initial vowels. No contracting in gen.; ως in sg. gen. for -ι and -ευ nouns. The usual α is not in acc. for -ι and –υ nouns.

ADJECTIVES: Spelled Like the Nouns They Describe

An adjective matches the noun it describes in gender, number, and case (a.k.a. G-N-C agreement). An adjective can be in written in several different positions relative to the noun it describes.

Position	Structure*		Translation
Attributive	1. ὁ ἀγαθὸς ἄνθρωπος	TAN	"the good man"
	2. ὁ ἄνθρωπος ὁ ἀγαθὸς	TNTA	
	3. ἄνθρωπος ὁ ἀγαθὸς	NTA	
	4. ἄνθρωπος ἀγαθὸς	NA	"good man"
Predicate	1. ἀγαθὸς [ἐστὶν] ὁ ἄνθρωπος	ATN	"The man is good."
	2. ὁ ἄνθρωπος [ἐστὶν] ἀγαθὸς	TNA	
Key: T = article, A = adjective, N = noun			

AAA Rule = Adjective preceded by an Article is Attributive.

An adjective can be used alone (or with its own article) as a noun (a.k.a. substantival use); e.g., τὰ ἀγαθά ("the good things").

Declension of Normal Vowel (2-1-2) Adjectives (like Second Decl. in masc. and neu., First Decl. in fem.)			
ἀγαθός — "good"			
	Masculine	Feminine	Neuter
SINGULAR Nom.	ἀγαθός	ἀγαθή	ἀγαθόν
Gen.	ἀγαθοῦ	ἀγαθῆς	ἀγαθοῦ
Dat.	ἀγαθῷ	ἀγαθῇ	ἀγαθῷ
Acc.	ἀγαθόν	ἀγαθήν	ἀγαθόν
PLURAL Nom.	ἀγαθοί	ἀγαθαί	ἀγαθά
Gen.	ἀγαθῶν	ἀγαθῶν	ἀγαθῶν
Dat.	ἀγαθοῖς	ἀγαθαῖς	ἀγαθοῖς
Acc.	ἀγαθούς	ἀγαθάς	ἀγαθά

Declension of "Old MacDonald" Adjectives
(2-1-2 adjectives with stems ending in ε, ι, or ρ "with α" in fem.)

μικρός — "small"

		Masculine	Feminine	Neuter
SINGULAR	Nom.	μικρός	μικρά	μικρόν
	Gen.	μικροῦ	μικρᾶς	μικροῦ
	Dat.	μικρῷ	μικρᾷ	μικρῷ
	Acc.	μικρόν	μικράν	μικρόν
PLURAL	Nom.	μικροί	μικραί	μικρά
	Gen.	μικρῶν	μικρῶν	μικρῶν
	Dat.	μικροῖς	μικραῖς	μικροῖς
	Acc.	μικρούς	μικράς	μικρά

Declension of Consonant Ending (3-3) Adjectives
(like Third Decl. in masc./fem. and Third Decl. in neu.)

		Liquid Type		-ς Types	
		Masc./Fem.	Neu.	Masc./Fem.	Neu.
SINGULAR	Nom.	πλείων	πλεῖον	ἀληθής	ἀληθές
	Gen.	πλείονος	πλείονος	ἀληθοῦς	ἀληθοῦς
	Dat.	πλείονι	πλείονι	ἀληθεῖ	ἀληθεῖ
	Acc.	πλείονα	πλεῖον	ἀληθῆ	ἀληθές
PLURAL	Nom.	πλείονες	πλείονα	ἀληθεῖς	ἀληθῆ
	Gen.	πλειόνων	πλειόνων	ἀληθῶν	ἀληθῶν
	Dat.	πλείοσι(ν)	πλείοσι(ν)	ἀληθέσι(ν)	ἀληθέσι(ν)
	Acc.	πλείονας	πλείονα	ἀληθεῖς	ἀληθῆ

Declension of -ντ Stem (3-1-3) Adjectives
(like Third Decl. in masc. and neu., First Decl. in fem.)

		Masculine	Feminine	Neuter
SINGULAR	Nom.	πᾶς	πᾶσα	πᾶν
	Gen.	παντός	πάσης	παντός
	Dat.	παντί	πάσῃ	παντί
	Acc.	πάντα	πᾶσαν	πᾶν
PLURAL	Nom.	πάντες	πᾶσαι	πάντα
	Gen.	πάντων	πασῶν	πάντων
	Dat.	πᾶσι	πάσαις	πᾶσι
	Acc.	πάντας	πάσας	πάντα

Note: πᾶς ("all, every") and ὅλος ("whole") are the two adjectives that are always in predicate position but translated as if in attributive position.

Adjectival Comparisons *

EXAMPLE ONE

Positive (declined as above)	σοφός	wise
Comparative (-τερος, -τερα, -τερον)	σοφώτερος	wiser
Superlative (-τατος, -τατη, -τατον)	σοφώτατος	most wise

EXAMPLE TWO

Positive (declined as above)	κακός	evil, wicked
Comparative (-ιων)	κακίων	more evil
Superlative (-ιστος)	κάκιστος	most evil

OTHER IRREGULARITIES

ἀγαθός	good	κρείσσων	better
κακός	evil, wicked	χείρων	worse
μέγας	great	μείζων	greater
πολύς	much, many	πλείων	more

*The comparative and superlative forms are declined like the positive form of the adjective following the appropriate 2-1-2, 3-3, or 3-1-3 declension. Sometimes comparative and superlative forms are used with elative meaning (e.g., "*very* small").

ADVERBS: Adding Information to the Verb

Just as many English adverbs are formed by adding "-ly" to an adjective, many NT Greek adverbs are formed by adding "-ως" to an adjective. Think of the forms as built off the adjective's genitive plural ending with a ς replacing the final ν.

Adjective		Genitive Plural	Adverb	
δίκαιος	just, righteous	δικαίων	δικαιώς	justly
καλός	good, beautiful	καλῶν	καλῶς	well
κακός	evil, wicked	κακῶν	κακῶς	wickedly

Similar to English, Greek adverbs can be used to describe actions comparatively and superlatively. The neuter accusative singular of the comparative *adjective* form is used for the comparative adverb; the neuter accusative plural of the superlative *adjective* form is used for the superlative adverb.

Positive Adverb		Comparative Adverb		Superlative Adverb	
δικαιώς	justly	δικαιότερον	more justly	δικαιότατα	most justly
καλώς	well	κάλλιον	better	κάλλιστα	best
κακῶς	wickedly	κακίον	more wickedly	κάκιστα	most wickedly

As with English, in addition to being described by adverbs, Greek verbs can be described by prepositional phrases, by infinitives, and by participles.

THE ARTICLE: Definitely THE One and Only

NT Greek has no indefinite article ("a") but has the definite article ("the"). Declining similarly to adjectives, its spelling must agree in gender, number, and case with the noun it modifies.

The Definite Article: "the"			
		Masculine	Feminine	Neuter
SINGULAR	Nom.	ὁ	ἡ	τό
	Gen.	τοῦ	τῆς	τοῦ
	Dat.	τῷ	τῇ	τῷ
	Acc.	τόν	τήν	τό
PLURAL	Nom.	οἱ	αἱ	τά
	Gen.	τῶν	τῶν	τῶν
	Dat.	τοῖς	ταῖς	τοῖς
	Acc.	τούς	τάς	τά

PRONOUNS: Noun Stand-ins

RELATIVE PRONOUN:
The basic pattern (without the rough breathing and accent marks) for all pronoun endings.

Relative Pronoun: "who, which, what, that"			
		Masculine	Feminine	Neuter
SINGULAR	Nom.	ὅς	ἥ	ὅ
	Gen.	οὗ	ἧς	οὗ
	Dat.	ᾧ	ᾗ	ᾧ
	Acc.	ὅν	ἥν	ὅ
PLURAL	Nom.	οἵ	αἵ	ἅ
	Gen.	ὧν	ὧν	ὧν
	Dat.	οἷς	αἷς	οἷς
	Acc.	οὕς	ἅς	ἅ

INTENSIVE PRONOUN: αὐτός (αὐτ + RELATIVE PRONOUN ENDINGS).

1. As an adjective in the predicate position:
   "him-/her-/it-self."

2. As an adjective in the attributive position: "the same."

3. Occurs most often as the third personal pronoun
   ("he/she/it").

DEMONSTRATIVE PRONOUNS:
The near (οὗτος, "this") and the far (ἐκεῖνος, "that") demonstratives follow the declension of the relative pronoun noted above, but the stem of οὗτος changes in the paradigm (note: if α or η is in the ending, then α is in the stem spelling instead of ο).

Near Demonstrative: "this"			
		Masculine	Feminine	Neuter
SINGULAR	Nom.	οὗτος	αὕτη	τοῦτο
	Gen.	τούτου	ταύτης	τούτου
	Dat.	τούτῳ	ταύτῃ	τούτῳ
	Accu.	τοῦτον	ταύτην	τοῦτο
PLURAL	Nom.	οὗτοι	αὗται	ταῦτα
	Gen.	τούτων	τούτων	τούτων
	Dat.	τούτοις	ταύταις	τούτοις
	Acc.	τούτους	ταύτας	ταῦτα

PERSONAL PRONOUNS: ἐγώ, σύ, αὐτός ("I," "YOU," "HE/SHE/IT").

1. The first and second personal pronouns have singular and
   plural case spellings but no gender differentiations.

2. The intensive pronoun αὐτός, in its various and gender
   differentiated forms (αὐτ + relative pronoun endings),
   serves as third person personal pronoun.

Personal Pronouns			
	FIRST PERSON	**SECOND PERSON**	**THIRD PERSON**
	"I, my, me"	"you, your"	"he, she, it"
SINGULAR Nom.	ἐγώ	σύ	
Gen.	ἐμοῦ (μου)	σου	The intensive
Dat.	ἐμοί (μοι)	σοι	pronoun αὐτός,
Acc.	ἐμέ (με)	σε	in its various
PLURAL Nom.	ἡμεῖς	ὑμεῖς	forms, serves
Gen.	ἡμῶν	ὑμῶν	here.
Dat.	ἡμῖν	ὑμῖν	
Acc.	ἡμᾶς	ὑμᾶς	

INTERROGATIVE PRONOUN: τίς, τί ("WHO?, WHICH?, WHAT?, WHY?").
The forms follow the third declension paradigm and all have an acute accent on the first syllable. They always occur in questions.

Interrogative Pronoun: "who?, which?, what?, why?"					
	Masc./Fem.	Neu.		Masc./Fem.	Neu.
SINGULAR Nom.	τίς	τί	**PLURAL** Nom.	τίνες	τίνα
Gen.	τίνος	τίνος	Gen.	τίνων	τίνων
Dat.	τίνι	τίνι	Dat.	τίσι(ν)	τίσι(ν)
Acc.	τίνα	τί	Acc.	τίνας	τίνα

INDEFINITE PRONOUN: τις, τι
("ANYONE/ANYTHING/SOMEONE/SOMETHING")
Its forms are all the same as the interrogative pronoun (above) except the mono-syllabic forms are rarely accented and the rest have ultima accents.

INDEFINITE RELATIVE PRONOUN: ὅστις, ἥτις, ὅτι
("WHOEVER, WHATEVER")
Is a compound word of ὅς + τις and both components are fully declined together as they are in their separate words.

Reflexive Pronouns:
Used to reference reflecting back to the self, there are no nominative forms for these pronouns.

1. The first person ἐμαυτοῦ ("myself") follows the declension of the intensive αὐτός with ἐμ- appended on the front of the forms.

2. The second person σεαυτοῦ ("yourself") follows the intensive αὐτός declension with σε- appended on the front of the forms.

3. The third person ἑαυτοῦ ("himself, herself, itself") follows the full αὐτός declension with ἑ- appended on the front of the forms.

4. The plural forms are the same for all persons, following the third person ἑαυτοῦ paradigm.

Reciprocal Pronoun: ἀλλήλων ("EACH OTHER, ONE ANOTHER").
Like the reflexive pronouns, there is no nominative form and it naturally occurs only in the plural (masc.): ἀλλήλων (gen.), ἀλλήλοις (dat.), ἀλλή-λους (acc.).

PREPOSITIONS: Pre-Positioned to Give Directions

Properly speaking, these small words can occur prefixed to verbs (e.g., ἐκ in ἐκβάλλω) and at the beginning of noun phrases in certain case forms. Most can be thought of in relation to a box.

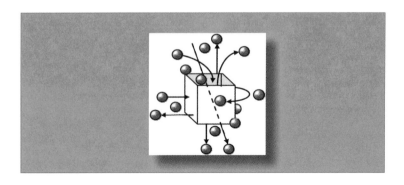

Prepositional Prefixes			
ἀμφί	around , on both sides	κατά	against, down (gen./acc.)
ἀνά	up, again (acc.)	μετά	with (gen.), after (acc.)
ἀντί	instead (gen.)	παρά	beside, at (gen./dat./acc.)
ἀπό	away, from (gen.)	περί	around, about (gen./acc.)
διά	through (gen./acc.)	πρό	before, in front of (gen.)
εἰς	into (acc.)	πρός	to, toward, with (acc.)
ἐκ	out of (gen.)	σύν	with, together (dat.)
ἐν	in, by (dat.)	ὑπέρ	over, beyond (gen./acc.)
ἐπί	on, upon (gen./dat./acc.)	ὑπό	under (gen./acc.)

The NT uses 43 other words that grammarians call "improper preposi-tions." While not occurring as prefixes, these can be used as prepositions or as adverbs and are sometimes referred to as "prepositional adverbs" or "adverbial prepositions." Included in this group are ἄχρι ("until, as far as"), ἐγγύς ("near"), ἐνώπιον ("before, in the presence/judgment of"), ἔξω ("outside"), ἕως ("until, up to"), μέσος ("in the middle of"), πλήν ("except for"), and χωρίς ("apart from, without").

VERBS: Used by the Author to Portray His View of the Action

INTRODUCTION: GREEK VERB BASICS

A verb's spelling varies to show such things as its role in the sentence (e.g., main verb or subordinate verb), its relationship to the subject of the sentence (e.g., done by or to the subject), and/or the author's view of the action (e.g., as a process, simple action, or state). A verb is "parsed" to describe these features of the verb's spelling: tense, voice, mood, person, and number (*"A **tense voice** shows the **mood** of a **person** in a **number** of ways."*). These five features can be described as follows:

1. Tense. English verb tenses have a time-based orientation (past/present/future) and some other languages have a kind-of-action tense system (linear/punctiliar); both of these systems base tense-form selection on the historic action itself. In NT Greek, however, tense-form selection is based primarily upon the way the author wishes to think about the action, the *aspect* he chooses to focus on. The other features of time and kind-of-action are portrayed by the lexical value of the term and the context, not in the verb's spelling (see also the "Verb Usage Guide" below in Part 2: Syntax).

   - Present: The action is being viewed as a *process* with *proximity*.

   - Imperfect: The action is being viewed as a process, with some *remoteness*, usually a temporal remoteness = in the past.

   - Future: The action is being viewed as a *whole* with anticipatory *proximity*, usually in the future.

   - Aorist: The action is being viewed as a *whole* with *remoteness*, often a temporal remoteness = in the past.

   - Perfect: The action is being viewed as a *state* with *proximity*.

   - Pluperfect: The action is being viewed as a *state* with some *remoteness*, usually a temporal remoteness = in the past.

2. Voice. Describes the subject's relation to the verbal action: *active*—doing or causing the action, *middle*—both doing and receiving the action, *passive*—receiving the action.

3. Mood. Describes the author's portrayal of the verbal action's actuality (*indicative*), potentiality (*subjunctive*), possibility (*optative*), or intentionality (*imperative*). Rather than mood, some forms serve other functions: verbal adjective (*participle*) and verbal noun (*infinitive*).

4. Person. Reflects who reportedly performs the verb (*first person* = "I, we"; *second person* = "you"; *third person* = "he/she/it, they") and typically matches (is in "concord" with) the subject.

5. Number. The verb usually matches (is in "concord" with) the singleness or plurality of the subject doing the action. Exceptions: neuter plural subjects, compound subjects, and indefinite plural subjects use singular verbs.

These parsing features are disclosed in various parts of the verb's spelling. The basic verb λύω ("I loose"), in its most fully dressed form, is ἐλελύκειμεν ("I had loosed"). The format portions and the features they disclose can be described as follows:

ἐ—λε—λύ—κ—ει—μεν		
ἐ	Augment	Imperfect, Aorist, and Pluperfect tenses, in indicative mood only; ε for verbs with an initial consonant; the vowel is lengthened for verbs with an initial vowel (α/ε → η; ι/υ → ῑ/ῡ; ο → ω; αι/ᾳ → η; οι → ῳ).
λε	Reduplication	Perfect and Pluperfect tenses (and some irregular verbs); verbs with an initial vowel merely augment; verbs with an initial double consonant or ζ, ξ, ψ, ρ merely augment with ε; verbs with initial θ, χ, or φ reduplicate with τ, κ, or π, respectively.
λύ	Verb Stem	The foundational core of the verb, which is said to contain the lexical value (or definitional meaning) of the word.
κ	Tense Indicator	This letter (along with the subsequent vowel) helps identify the tense: σ = Future; σα = Aorist; κα = Perfect; κει = Pluperfect; θη = Future and Aorist passive; no tense indicator in mid./pass. of Perfect and Pluperfect, nor in second Aorist and second Perfect forms, which change the verb stem instead.
ει	Connecting Vowel	Usually ο before μ and ν, but ε elsewhere; ω/η in subjunctive; οι/αι in optative.
μεν	Personal Ending	Voice (active, middle, passive), Person (first, second, third), and Number (singular, plural). See the following personal ending charts.

Primary Personal Endings (present, future, perfect)				Secondary Personal Endings (aorist, imperfect, pluperfect)			
ACTIVE VOICE (some exceptions)				**ACTIVE VOICE** (some exceptions)			
	SINGULAR		PLURAL		SINGULAR		PLURAL
1st	ω	1st	-μεν	1st	-ν	1st	-μεν
2nd	-εις	2nd	-τε	2nd	-ς	2nd	-τε
3rd	-ει	3rd	-σι(ν)	3rd	-ε(ν)	3rd	-ν
MIDDLE/PASSIVE VOICES (2nd sing. regularly shortened to η)				**MIDDLE/PASSIVE VOICES** (2nd sing. regularly drops the σ and contracts the vowels; other exceptions in Aorist)			
	SINGULAR		PLURAL		SINGULAR		PLURAL
1st	-μαι	1st	-μεθα	1st	-μην	1st	-μεθα
2nd	-σαι	2nd	-σθε	2nd	-σο	2nd	-σθε
3rd	-ται	3rd	-νται	3rd	-το	3rd	-ντο

Verb form paradigm charts can be organized by tenses, by moods, or by "principal parts." The six principal parts—(1) Present, (2) Future, (3) Aorist-Active, (4) Perfect, (5) Perfect-Middle/Passive, and (6) Aorist-Passive—form a way to remember key spelling variations in the various paradigms. Many grammar texts outline the principal parts for the most irregular NT verbs (cf. pp. 51-52 below). For the most complete listing for all NT verbs and their occurring principal parts, see Warren C. Trenchard, *Complete Vocabulary Guide to the Greek New Testament* (Grand Rapids: Zondervan, 1998), 237–72. Instead of by principal parts, the following model paradigms are organized by mood and tense so as to highlight the similarities in the personal endings as another way to remember the verb forms. The two main paradigm sets use the terms λύω ("I loose") and δίδωμι ("I give").

ω **CONJUGATION:** PRESENT ACTIVE INDICATIVE FIRST SINGULAR ENDING IN ω

See charts that follow.

INDICATIVE MOOD for ω VERBS

	Present Tense stem + vowel + primary endings	Imperfect Tense ἐ + stem + vowel + secondary endings
	Active Voice "I loose"	**Active Voice** "I was loosing"
SINGULAR 1st	λύω	ἔλυον
2nd	λύεις	ἔλυες
3rd	λύει	ἔλυε(ν)
PLURAL 1st	λύομεν	ἐλύομεν
2nd	λύετε	ἐλύετε
3rd	λύουσι(ν)	ἔλυον
	Middle/Passive Voice "I am loosed"	**Middle/Passive Voice** "I was being loosed"
SINGULAR 1st	λύομαι	ἐλυόμην
2nd	λύῃ	ἐλύου
3rd	λύεται	ἐλύετο
PLURAL 1st	λυόμεθα	ἐλυόμεθα
2nd	λύεσθε	ἐλύεσθε
3rd	λύονται	ἐλύοντο

INDICATIVE MOOD for ω VERBS (continued)

Future Tense
stem + σ / θησ + vowel + primary endings

Active Voice "I will loose"

SINGULAR	1st	λύσω	PLURAL	1st	λύσομεν
	2nd	λύσεις		2nd	λύσετε
	3rd	λύσει		3rd	λύσουσι(ν)

Middle Voice "I will loose myself"

SINGULAR	1st	λύσομαι	PLURAL	1st	λυσόμεθα
	2nd	λύσῃ		2nd	λύσεσθε
	3rd	λύσεται		3rd	λύσονται

Passive Voice "I will be loosed"

SINGULAR	1st	λυθήσομαι	PLURAL	1st	λυθησόμεθα
	2nd	λυθήσῃ		2nd	λυθήσεσθε
	3rd	λυθήσεται		3rd	λυθήσονται

1st Aorist Tense
ἐ + stem + σα / θη + secondary endings
[2nd Aorist → ἐ + modified stem + secondary endings]

Active Voice "I loosed"

SINGULAR	1st	ἔλυσα	PLURAL	1st	ἐλύσαμεν
	2nd	ἔλυσας		2nd	ἐλύσατε
	3rd	ἔλυσε(ν)		3rd	ἔλυσαν

Middle Voice "I loosed myself"

SINGULAR	1st	ἐλυσάμην	PLURAL	1st	ἐλυσάμεθα
	2nd	ἐλύσω		2nd	ἐλύσασθε
	3rd	ἐλύσατο		3rd	ἐλύσαντο

Passive Voice "I was loosed"

SINGULAR	1st	ἐλύθην	PLURAL	1st	ἐλύθημεν
	2nd	ἐλύθης		2nd	ἐλύθητε
	3rd	ἐλύθη		3rd	ἐλύθησαν

INDICATIVE MOOD for ω VERBS (continued)

PERFECT TENSE
redup. + stem + κα/- + primary endings

ACTIVE VOICE "I have loosed"

	SINGULAR		PLURAL
1st	λέλυκα	1st	λελύκαμεν
2nd	λέλυκας	2nd	λελύκατε
3rd	λέλυκε(ν)	3rd	λελύκασι(ν) or λέλυκαν

MIDDLE/PASSIVE VOICE "I have been loosed"

	SINGULAR		PLURAL
1st	λέλυμαι	1st	λελύμεθα
2nd	λέλυσαι	2nd	λέλυσθε
3rd	λέλυται	3rd	λέλυνται

PLUPERFECT TENSE
ἐ + redup. + stem + κει/- + secondary endings

ACTIVE VOICE "I had loosed"

	SINGULAR		PLURAL
1st	ἐλελύκειν	1st	ἐλελύκειμεν
2nd	ἐλελύκεις	2nd	ἐλελύκειτε
3rd	ἐλελύκει	3rd	ἐλελύκεισαν

MIDDLE/PASSIVE VOICE "I had been loosed"

	SINGULAR		PLURAL
1st	ἐλελύμην	1st	ἐλελύμεθα
2nd	ἐλέλυσο	2nd	ἐλέλυσθε
3rd	ἐλέλυτο	3rd	ἐλέλυντο

SUBJUNCTIVE MOOD for ω VERBS

PRESENT TENSE
stem + lengthened vowel + primary endings

ACTIVE VOICE — "I would be loosing"

	SINGULAR		PLURAL
1st	λύω	1st	λύωμεν
2nd	λύῃς	2nd	λύητε
3rd	λύῃ	3rd	λύωσι(ν)

MIDDLE/PASSIVE VOICE — "I would be loosed"

	SINGULAR		PLURAL
1st	λύωμαι	1st	λυώμεθα
2nd	λύῃ	2nd	λύησθε
3rd	λύηται	3rd	λύωνται

1ST AORIST TENSE
Present subjunctive forms (as in chart at left) + σ/θ
[2nd Aorist → modified stem]

ACTIVE VOICE — "I would loose"

	SINGULAR		PLURAL
1st	λύσω	1st	λύσωμεν
2nd	λύσῃς	2nd	λύσητε
3rd	λύσῃ	3rd	λύσωσι(ν)

MIDDLE VOICE — "I would loose myself"

	SINGULAR		PLURAL
1st	λύσωμαι	1st	λυσώμεθα
2nd	λύσῃ	2nd	λύσησθε
3rd	λύσηται	3rd	λύσωνται

PASSIVE VOICE — "I would be loosed"

	SINGULAR		PLURAL
1st	λυθῶ	1st	λυθῶμεν
2nd	λυθῇς	2nd	λυθῆτε
3rd	λυθῇ	3rd	λυθῶσι(ν)

The Subjunctive mood occurs primarily in the Present and Aorist tenses (there are only 10 Perfect tense subjunctives in the NT; all are forms of οἶδα). The Aorist passive forms copy the Aorist active forms with θ instead of σ.

IMPERATIVE MOOD for ω VERBS

PRESENT TENSE
stem + vowel + specialized endings

ACTIVE VOICE—"You be loosing"

	SINGULAR		PLURAL
2nd	λῦε		λύετε
3rd	λυέτω		λυέτωσαν

MIDDLE/PASSIVE VOICE—"You be loosed"

	SINGULAR		PLURAL
2nd	λύου		λύεσθε
3rd	λυέσθω		λυέσθωσαν

1ST AORIST TENSE
stem + σα /θη + specialized endings
[2nd Aorist → modified stem + specialized endings]

ACTIVE VOICE—"You loose"

	SINGULAR		PLURAL
2nd	λῦσον		λύσατε
3rd	λυσάτω		λυσάτωσαν

MIDDLE VOICE—"You loose yourself"

	SINGULAR		PLURAL
2nd	λῦσαι		λύσασθε
3rd	λυσάσθω		λυσάσθωσαν

PASSIVE VOICE—"You be loosed"

	SINGULAR		PLURAL
2nd	λύθητι		λύθητε
3rd	λυθήτω		λυθήτωσαν

The Imperative mood occurs primarily in the Present and Aorist tenses (the NT has only 4 occurrences of Perfect tense imperatives). No first person forms. The second person plural forms mimic the indicative.

OPTATIVE MOOD for ω VERBS

Active Voice

		1st	-μι
SINGULAR		2nd	-ς
		3rd	---
		1st	-μεν
PLURAL		2nd	-τε
		3rd	-εν

Middle/Passive Voice

		1st	-μην
SINGULAR		2nd	-ο
		3rd	-το
		1st	-μεθα
PLURAL		2nd	-σθε
		3rd	-ντο

The Optative mood is used less than 70 times in the NT. Regularly exhibits οι or οι αι as the connecting vowel (ει = Aorist passive) with the other usual tense and voice indicators.

INFINITIVE for ω VERBS

VOICE	PRESENT	FUTURE	1ST AORIST	2ND AORIST	PERFECT
ACTIVE	λύειν	λύσειν	λῦσαι	βαλεῖν	λελυκέναι
MIDDLE	λύεσθαι	λύσεσθαι	λύσασθαι	βαλέσθαι	λελύσθαι
PASSIVE	λύεσθαι	λυθήσεσθαι	λυθῆναι	βληθῆναι	λελύσθαι

All forms end in either -ειν (for contract verbs, -αν or -ουν) or -αι; all middle/passive forms end in -σθαι except the Aorist passive, which is always -ναι. The usual tense and voice indicators are used. As a verb, the infinitive can have a subject (always in accusative case). As a noun, it can have an article (neuter).

PARTICIPLE for ω VERBS

PRESENT TENSE

			Masculine	Feminine	Neuter
ACTIVE	SINGULAR	Nom.	λύων	λύουσα	λῦον
		Gen.	λύοντος	λυούσης	λύοντος
		Dat.	λύοντι	λυούσῃ	λύοντι
		Acc.	λύοντα	λύουσαν	λῦον
	PLURAL	Nom.	λύοντες	λύουσαι	λύοντα
		Gen.	λυόντων	λυουσῶν	λυόντων
		Dat.	λύουσι(ν)	λυούσαις	λύουσι(ν)
		Acc.	λύοντας	λυούσας	λύοντα

Declines like πᾶς (except for the sing. nom. form) and provides the pattern for active (and Aorist passive) participles in other tenses.

PARTICIPLE for ω VERBS (continued)

PRESENT TENSE

		Masculine	Feminine	Neuter
MIDDLE/ PASSIVE SINGULAR	Nom.	λυόμενος	λυομένη	λυόμενον
	Gen.	λυομένου	λυομένης	λυομένου
	Dat.	λυομένῳ	λυομένῃ	λυομένῳ
	Acc.	λυόμενον	λυομένην	λυόμενον
PLURAL	Nom.	λυόμενοι	λυόμεναι	λυόμενα
	Gen.	λυομένων	λυομένων	λυομένων
	Dat.	λυομένοις	λυομέναις	λυομένοις
	Acc.	λυομένους	λυομένας	λυόμενα

Declines like ἀγαθός with -ομεν- inserted and provides the pattern for middle/passive participles in other tenses (except for Aorist passive).

PARTICIPLE for ω VERBS: Other Tenses				
		FUTURE TENSE		
		Masculine	Feminine	Neuter
ACTIVE	SINGULAR	Nom.	λύσων	λύσουσα	λῦσον
		Gen.	λύσοντος	λυσούσης	λύσοντος
MIDDLE		Nom.	λυσόμενος	λυσομένη	λυσόμενον
		Gen.	λυσομένου	λυσομενης	λυσομένου
PASSIVE		Nom.	λυθησόμενος	λυθησομένη	λυθησόμενον
		Gen.	λυθησομένου	λυθησομένης	λυθησομένου
		AORIST TENSE		
ACTIVE	SINGULAR	Nom.	λύσας	λύσασα	λῦσαν
		Gen.	λύσαντος	λυσάσης	λύσαντος
MIDDLE		Nom.	λυσάμενος	λυσαμένη	λυσάμενον
		Gen.	λυσαμένου	λυσαμένης	λυσαμένου
PASSIVE		Nom.	λυθείς	λυθεῖσα	λυθέν
		Gen.	λυθέντος	λυθείσης	λυθέντος
		PERFECT TENSE		
ACTIVE	SINGULAR	Nom.	λελυκώς	λελυκυῖα	λελυκός
		Gen.	λελυκότος	λελυκυίας	λελυκότος
MID./ PASS.		Nom.	λελυμένος	λελυμένη	λελυμένον
		Gen.	λελυμένου	λελυμένης	λελυμένου

μι **CONJUGATION:** PRESENT ACTIVE INDICATIVE FIRST SINGULAR ENDING IN μι

These verbs have reduplication in the Present and Imperfect tenses (as well as Perfect and Pluperfect), often lengthened stem vowels (so the stems can be difficult to recognize), and absent connecting vowels (in Present, Imperfect, and some middle-passive forms). See the following charts.

INDICATIVE MOOD for μι VERBS

PRESENT TENSE
redup. + stem + modified primary endings

ACTIVE VOICE — "I give"

		SINGULAR			PLURAL
1st	δίδωμι		1st	δίδομεν
2nd	δίδως		2nd	δίδοτε
3rd	δίδωσι(ν)		3rd	διδόασι(ν)

MIDDLE/PASSIVE VOICE — "I am given"

		SINGULAR			PLURAL
1st	δίδομαι		1st	διδόμεθα
2nd	δίδοσαι		2nd	δίδοσθε
3rd	δίδοται		3rd	δίδονται

IMPERFECT TENSE
ἐ + redup. + stem + vowel + secondary endings

ACTIVE VOICE — "I was giving"

		SINGULAR			PLURAL
1st	ἐδίδουν		1st	ἐδίδομεν
2nd	ἐδίδους		2nd	ἐδίδοτε
3rd	ἐδίδου		3rd	ἐδίδοσαν

MIDDLE/PASSIVE VOICE — "I was being given"

		SINGULAR			PLURAL
1st	ἐδιδόμην		1st	ἐδιδόμεθα
2nd	ἐδίδοσο		2nd	ἐδίδοσθε
3rd	ἐδίδοτο		3rd	ἐδίδοντο

INDICATIVE MOOD for μι VERBS (continued)

Future Tense
stem + σ / θησ + vowel + primary endings

Active Voice "I will give"

SINGULAR	1st	δώσω
	2nd	δώσεις
	3rd	δώσει
PLURAL	1st	δώσομεν
	2nd	δώσετε
	3rd	δώσουσι(ν)

Middle Voice "I will give myself"

SINGULAR	1st	δώσομαι
	2nd	δώση
	3rd	δώσεται
PLURAL	1st	δωσόμεθα
	2nd	δώσεσθε
	3rd	δώσονται

Passive Voice "I will be given"

SINGULAR	1st	δοθήσομαι
	2nd	δοθήση
	3rd	δοθήσεται
PLURAL	1st	δοθησόμεθα
	2nd	δοθήσεσθε
	3rd	δοθήσονται

2nd Aorist Tense
ἐ + stem + κα /-/θη + secondary endings
[1st Aorist → ἐ + stem + σα / θη) + secondary endings]

Active Voice "I gave"

SINGULAR	1st	ἔδωκα
	2nd	ἔδωκας
	3rd	ἔδωκε(ν)
PLURAL	1st	ἐδώκαμεν
	2nd	ἐδώκατε
	3rd	ἔδωκαν

Middle Voice "I gave myself"

SINGULAR	1st	ἐδόμην
	2nd	ἔδου
	3rd	ἔδοτο
PLURAL	1st	ἐδόμεθα
	2nd	ἔδοσθε
	3rd	ἔδοντο

Passive Voice "I was given"

SINGULAR	1st	ἐδόθην
	2nd	ἐδόθης
	3rd	ἐδόθη
PLURAL	1st	ἐδόθημεν
	2nd	ἐδόθητε
	3rd	ἐδόθησαν

INDICATIVE MOOD for μι VERBS (continued)

PERFECT TENSE
redup.(ε) + stem + κα/- + primary endings

ACTIVE VOICE "I have given"

	SINGULAR		PLURAL
1st	δέδωκα	1st	δεδώκαμεν
2nd	δέδωκας	2nd	δεδώκατε
3rd	δέδωκε(ν)	3rd	δεδώκασι(ν)

MIDDLE/PASSIVE VOICE "I have been given"

	SINGULAR		PLURAL
1st	δέδομαι	1st	δεδόμεθα
2nd	δέδοσαι	2nd	δέδοσθε
3rd	δέδοται	3rd	δέδονται

PLUPERFECT TENSE
ἐ + redup.(ε) + stem + κει/- + secondary endings

ACTIVE VOICE "I had given"

	SINGULAR		PLURAL
1st	ἐδεδώκειν	1st	ἐδεδώκειμεν
2nd	ἐδεδώκεις	2nd	ἐδεδώκειτε
3rd	ἐδεδώκει	3rd	ἐδεδώκεισαν

MIDDLE/PASSIVE VOICE "I had been given"

	SINGULAR		PLURAL
1st	ἐδεδόμην	1st	ἐδεδόμεθα
2nd	ἐδέδοσο	2nd	ἐδέδοσθε
3rd	ἐδέδοτο	3rd	ἐδέδοντο

SUBJUNCTIVE MOOD for μι VERBS

Present Tense
redup. + stem + long vowel + primary endings

Active Voice — "I would be giving"

SINGULAR	1st	διδῶ	PLURAL	1st	διδῶμεν
	2nd	διδῷς		2nd	διδῶτε
	3rd	διδῷ		3rd	διδῶσι(ν)

Middle/Passive Voice — "I would be given"

SINGULAR	1st	διδῶμαι	PLURAL	1st	διδώμεθα
	2nd	διδῷ		2nd	διδῶσθε
	3rd	διδῶται		3rd	διδῶνται

2nd Aorist Tense
Present subjunctive forms (as in chart at left) with no redup. [1st Aorist→ exhibits σα in active and middle]

Active Voice — "I would give"

SINGULAR	1st	δῶ	PLURAL	1st	δῶμεν
	2nd	δῷς		2nd	δῶτε
	3rd	δῷ		3rd	δῶσι(ν)

Middle Voice — "I would give myself"

SINGULAR	1st	δῶμαι	PLURAL	1st	δώμεθα
	2nd	δῷ		2nd	δῶσθε
	3rd	δῶται		3rd	δῶνται

Passive Voice — "I would be given"

SINGULAR	1st	δοθῶ	PLURAL	1st	δοθῶμεν
	2nd	δοθῇς		2nd	δοθῆτε
	3rd	δοθῇ		3rd	δοθῶσι(ν)

The Subjunctive mood occurs only in the Present and Aorist tenses. The Aorist passive forms are like Aorist passive subjunctives in ω verbs: stem + θ + long vowel + primary endings (see for λύω on page 30 above).

IMPERATIVE MOOD for μι VERBS

PRESENT TENSE
redup. + stem + ω verb imperative endings

ACTIVE VOICE "You be giving"

	SINGULAR		PLURAL
2nd	δίδου	2nd	δίδοτε
3rd	διδότω	3rd	διδότωσαν

MIDDLE/PASSIVE VOICE "You be given"

	SINGULAR		PLURAL
2nd	δίδοσο	2nd	δίδοσθε
3rd	διδόσθω	3rd	διδόσθωσαν

2ND AORIST TENSE
Present imperative forms with no redup.
[1st Aorist→ exhibits σα in active and middle]

ACTIVE VOICE "You give"

	SINGULAR		PLURAL
2nd	δός	2nd	δότε
3rd	δότω	3rd	δότωσαν

MIDDLE VOICE "You give yourself"

	SINGULAR		PLURAL
2nd	δοῦ	2nd	δόσθε
3rd	δόσθω	3rd	δόσθωσαν

PASSIVE VOICE "You be given"

	SINGULAR		PLURAL
2nd	δόθητι	2nd	δόθητε
3rd	δοθήτω	3rd	δοθήτωσαν

Endings are similar to those in ω verb imperatives (except 2nd person singular). The Present tense 2nd person plural forms mimic the indicative.

OPTATIVE MOOD for μι VERBS

		ACTIVE VOICE				MIDDLE/PASSIVE VOICE	
SINGULAR	1st	-ιην	PLURAL	1st	-ιημεν		
	2nd	-ιης		2nd	-ιητε		
	3rd	-ιη		3rd	-ιησαν		

	SINGULAR			PLURAL	
1st	-ιμην	1st	-ιμεθα		
2nd	-ιο	2nd	-ισθε		
3rd	-ιτο	3rd	-ιντο		

The Optative mood is used less than 70 times in the NT. Regularly exhibits -οι- as the connecting vowel with the other usual tense and voice indicators.

INFINITIVE for μι VERBS

VOICE	PRESENT	FUTURE	2ND AORIST	PERFECT
ACTIVE	δίδόναι	δώσειν	δοῦναι	δεδωκέναι
MIDDLE	δίδοσθαι	δώσεσθαι	δόσθαι	δεδόσθαι
PASSIVE	δίδοσθαι	δοθήσεσθαι	δοθῆναι	δεδόσθαι

All forms end in either -ειν or -αι; all middle/passive forms end in -σθαι except the Aorist passive, which is always -ναι. The usual tense and voice indicators are used. As a verb, the infinitive can have a subject (always in accusative case). As a noun, it can have an article (neuter).

PARTICIPLE for μι VERBS

Present Tense

		Masculine	Feminine	Neuter	
ACTIVE	SINGULAR — Nom.	διδούς	διδοῦσα	διδόν	Declines like πᾶς and provides the pattern for active (and Aorist passive) participles in other tenses.
	Gen.	διδόντος	διδούσης	διδόντος	
	Dat.	διδόντι	διδούσῃ	διδόντι	
	Acc.	διδόντα	διδοῦσαν	διδόν	
	PLURAL — Nom.	διδόντες	διδοῦσαι	διδόντα	
	Gen.	διδόντων	διδουσῶν	διδόντων	
	Dat.	διδοῦσι(ν)	διδούσαις	διδοῦσι(ν)	
	Acc.	διδόντας	διδούσας	διδόντα	
Middle/ Passive	SINGULAR — Nom.	διδόμενος	διδομένη	διδόμενον	Declines like ἀγαθός with -μεν- inserted and provides the pattern for middle/ passive participles in other tenses (except the Aorist passive).
	Gen.	διδομένου	διδομένης	διδομένου	
	Dat.	διδομένῳ	διδομένῃ	διδομένῳ	
	Acc.	διδόμενον	διδομένην	διδόμενον	
	PLURAL — Nom.	διδόμενοι	διδόμεναι	διδόμενα	
	Gen.	διδομένων	διδομένων	διδομένων	
	Dat.	διδομένοις	διδομέναις	διδομένοις	
	Acc.	διδομένους	διδομένας	διδόμενα	

PARTICIPLE for μι VERBS: Other Tenses				
			FUTURE TENSE		
			Masculine	Feminine	Neuter
ACTIVE	SINGULAR	Nom.	δώσων	δωσοῦσα	δῶσον
		Gen.	δωσόντος	δωσούσης	δωσόντος
MIDDLE		Nom.	δωσόμενος	δωσομένη	δωσόμενον
		Gen.	δωσομένου	δωσομένης	δωσομένου
PASSIVE		Nom.	δωθησόμενος	δωθησομένα	δωθησόμενον
		Gen.	δωθησομένου	δωθησομένης	δωθησομένου
			2ND AORIST Tense [1ST AORIST → σα]		
ACTIVE	SINGULAR	Nom.	δούς	δοῦσα	δόν
		Gen.	δόντος	δούσης	δόντος
MIDDLE		Nom.	δόμενος	δομένη	δόμενον
		Gen.	δομένου	δομένης	δομένου
PASSIVE		Nom.	δοθείς	δοθεῖσα	δοθέν
		Gen.	δοθέντος	δοθείσης	δοθέντος
			PERFECT TENSE		
ACTIVE	SINGULAR	Nom.	δεδωκώς	δεδωκυῖα	δεδωκός
		Gen.	δεδωκότος	δεδωκυίας	δεδωκότος
MID./ PASS.		Nom.	δεδομένος	δεδομένη	δεδόμενον
		Gen.	δεδομένου	δεδομένης	δεδομένου

CONTRACT VERBS: STEMS ENDING IN α, ε, OR ο

Verb stems ending in a vowel contract with the connecting vowels of the personal endings of the ω conjugation in the Present and Imperfect tenses (the vowel lengthens before the consonant indicators of the other tenses: σ or κ). See the vowel contraction chart on page 13.

CONTRACT VERBS: PRESENT TENSE INDICATIVE

Standard Endings: Active/Middle-Passive			ACTIVE VOICE			MIDDLE/PASSIVE VOICE		
			τιμάω "I honor" τιμα-	φιλέω "I love" φιλε-	δηλόω "I show" δηλο-	τιμάω "I honor" τιμα-	φιλέω "I love" φιλε-	δηλόω "I show" δηλο-
SINGULAR	1st	-ω/-ομαι	τιμῶ	φιλῶ	δηλῶ	τιμῶμαι	φιλοῦμαι	δηλοῦμαι
	2nd	-εις/-ῃ	τιμᾷς	φιλεῖς	δηλοῖς	τιμᾷ	φιλῇ	δηλοῖ
	3rd	-ει/-εται	τιμᾷ	φιλεῖ	δηλοῖ	τιμᾶται	φιλεῖται	δηλοῦται
PLURAL	1st	-ομεν/-ομεθα	τιμῶμεν	φιλοῦμεν	δηλοῦμεν	τιμώμεθα	φιλούμεθα	δηλούμεθα
	2nd	-ετε/-εσθε	τιμᾶτε	φιλεῖτε	δηλοῦτε	τιμᾶσθε	φιλεῖσθε	δηλοῦσθε
	3rd	-ουσι/-ονται	τιμῶσι(ν)	φιλοῦσι(ν)	δηλοῦσι(ν)	τιμῶνται	φιλοῦνται	δηλοῦνται

CONTRACT VERBS: PRESENT TENSE SUBJUNCTIVE

Standard Endings: Active/Middle-Passive		Active Voice			Middle/Passive Voice		
		τιμάω "I honor" τιμα-	φιλέω "I love" φιλε-	δηλόω "I show" δηλο-	τιμάω "I honor" τιμα-	φιλέω "I love" φιλε-	δηλόω "I show" δηλο-
SINGULAR	1st	-ω / -ωμαι	τιμῶ	φιλῶ	δηλῶ	τιμῶμαι	φιλῶμαι	δηλῶμαι
	2nd	-ῃς / -ῃ	τιμᾷς	φιλῇς	δηλοῖς	τιμᾷ	φιλῇ	δηλοῖ
	3rd	-ῃ / -ηται	τιμᾷ	φιλῇ	δηλοῖ	τιμᾶται	φιλῆται	δηλῶται
PLURAL	1st	-ωμεν / -ωμεθα	τιμῶμεν	φιλῶμεν	δηλῶμεν	τιμώμεθα	φιλώμεθα	δηλώμεθα
	2nd	-ητε / -ησθε	τιμᾶτε	φιλῆτε	δηλῶτε	τιμᾶσθε	φιλῆσθε	δηλῶσθε
	3rd	-ωσι(ν) / -ωνται	τιμῶσι(ν)	φιλῶσι(ν)	δηλῶσι(ν)	τιμῶνται	φιλῶνται	δηλῶνται

CONTRACT VERBS: PRESENT TENSE IMPERATIVE

	Standard Endings: Active/Middle-Passive	Active Voice τιμάω "I honor" τιμα-	φιλέω "I love" φιλε-	δηλόω "I show" δηλο-	Middle/Passive Voice τιμάω "I honor" τιμα-	φιλέω "I love" φιλε-	δηλόω "I show" δηλο-
SINGULAR 2nd	-ε/-ου	τίμα	φίλει	δήλου	τιμῶ	φιλοῦ	δηλοῦ
SINGULAR 3rd	-έτω/-έσθω	τιμάτω	φιλείτω	δηλούτω	τιμάσθω	φιλείσθω	δηλούσθω
PLURAL 2nd	-ετε/-εσθε	τιμᾶτε	φιλεῖτε	δηλοῦτε	τιμᾶσθε	φιλεῖσθε	δηλοῦσθε
PLURAL 3rd	-όντων/-έσθων	τιμώντων	φιλούντων	δηλούντων	τιμάσθων	φιλείσθων	δηλούσθων

CONTRACT VERBS: PRESENT TENSE INFINITIVE

Standard Endings: Active/Middle-Passive	Active Voice τιμάω "I honor" τιμα-	φιλέω "I love" φιλε-	δηλόω "I show" δηλο-	Middle/Passive Voice τιμάω "I honor" τιμα-	φιλέω "I love" φιλε-	δηλόω "I show" δηλο-
-ειν/-εσθαι	τιμᾶν	φιλεῖν	δηλοῦν	τιμᾶσθαι	φιλεῖσθαι	δηλοῦσθαι

CONTRACT VERBS: PRESENT TENSE PARTICIPLE

	Active Voice			Middle/Passive Voice		
	τιμάω "I honor" τιμα-	φιλέω "I love" φιλε-	δηλόω "I show" δηλο-	τιμάω "I honor" τιμα-	φιλέω "I love" φιλε-	δηλόω "I show" δηλο-
SINGULAR Masc. Nom.	τιμῶν	φιλῶν	δηλῶν	τιμώμενος	φιλούμενος	δηλούμενος
Fem. Nom.	τιμῶσα	φιλοῦσα	δηλοῦσα	τιμωμένη	φιλουμένη	δηλουμένη
Neu. Nom.	τιμῶν	φιλοῦν	δηλοῦν	τιμώμενον	φιλούμενον	δηλούμενον

CONTRACT VERBS: IMPERFECT TENSE INDICATIVE

	Standard Endings: Active/Middle-Passive	Active Voice			Middle/Passive Voice		
		τιμάω "I honor" τιμα-	φιλέω "I love" φιλε-	δηλόω "I show" δηλο-	τιμάω "I honor" τιμα-	φιλέω "I love" φιλε-	δηλόω "I show" δηλο-
SINGULAR 1st	-ον/-ομην	ἐτίμων	ἐφίλουν	ἐδήλουν	ἐτιμώμην	ἐφιλούμην	ἐδηλούμην
2nd	-ες/-ου	ἐτίμας	ἐφίλεις	ἐδήλους	ἐτιμῶ	ἐφιλοῦ	ἐδηλοῦ
3rd	-ε/-ετο	ἐτίμα	ἐφίλει	ἐδήλου	ἐτιμᾶτο	ἐφιλεῖτο	ἐδηλοῦτο
PLURAL 1st	-ομεν/-ομεθα	ἐτιμῶμεν	ἐφιλοῦμεν	ἐδηλοῦμεν	ἐτιμώμεθα	ἐφιλούμεθα	ἐδηλούμεθα
2nd	-ετε/-εσθε	ἐτιμᾶτε	ἐφιλεῖτε	ἐδηλοῦτε	ἐτιμᾶσθε	ἐφιλεῖσθε	ἐδηλοῦσθε
3rd	-ον/-οντο	ἐτίμων	ἐφίλουν	ἐδήλουν	ἐτιμῶντο	ἐφιλοῦντο	ἐδηλοῦντο

LIQUID VERBS: STEMS ENDING IN λ, μ, ν, OR ρ

Verb stems ending in a "liquid" consonant (λ, μ, ν, ρ) cannot stand next to the σ of the Future and Aorist tense indicators, so compensations are made. In the *Future tense* (-σ-) the σ is dropped but an ε is added to the stem and the verb is conjugated like the ε contract verbs above (see the vowel contraction chart on page 13). In the *Aorist tense* (-σα-) the σ is dropped and a short stem vowel preceding the liquid letter is often lengthened (many liquid verbs also lengthen the stem in the present tense).

LIQUID VERBS: INDICATIVE MOOD					
αἴρω ("I lift up")					
		PRESENT	FUTURE	AORIST	PERFECT
SINGULAR	1st	αἴρω	ἀρῶ	ἦρα	ἦρκα
	2nd	αἴρεις	ἀρεῖς	ἦρας	ἦρκας
	3rd	αἴρει	ἀρεῖ	ἦρε	ἦρκε(ν)
PLURAL	1st	αἴρομεν	ἀροῦμεν	ἤραμεν	ἤρκαμεν
	2nd	αἴρετε	ἀρεῖτε	ἤρατε	ἤρκατε
	3rd	αἴρουσι(ν)	ἀροῦσι(ν)	ἦραν	ἤρκασι(ν)
μένω ("I remain")					
		PRESENT	FUTURE	AORIST	PERFECT
SINGULAR	1st	μένω	μενῶ	ἔμεινα	μεμένηκα
	2nd	μένεις	μενεῖς	ἔμεινας	μεμένηκας
	3rd	μένει	μενεῖ	ἔμεινε	μεμένηκε(ν)
PLURAL	1st	μένομεν	μενοῦμεν	ἐμείναμεν	μεμενήκαμεν
	2nd	μένετε	μενεῖτε	ἐμείνατε	μεμενήκατε
	3rd	μένουσι(ν)	μενοῦσι(ν)	ἔμειναν	μεμενήκασι(ν)

MUTE ENDING VERBS: STEMS ENDING IN π, β, φ, κ, γ, χ, τ, δ, θ

Verb stems ending in a "mute" consonant (labials: π, β, φ; palatals: κ, γ, χ; dentals: τ, δ, θ) follow the contraction chart on page 13 above in forming the *Future and Aorist tenses* (+ σ), the *Perfect and Pluperfect tenses* (+ κ), and the *passive voices* (+ θ).

MUTE ENDING VERB: TENSE CONSONANT CHANGES

Present		Future	Aorist	Aorist Passive
ἀνοίγω	"I open"	ἀνοίξω	ἤνοιξα	ἠνοίχθην
διδάσκω	"I teach"	διδάξω	ἐδίδαξα	ἐδιδάχθην
πείθω	"I persuade"	πείσω	ἔπεισα	ἐπείσθην
διώκω	"I pursue"	διώξω	ἐδίωξα	ἐδιώχθην
στρέφω	"I turn"	στρέψω	ἔστρεψα	ἐστράφην
καλύπτω	"I cover"	καλύψω	ἐκάλυψα	ἐκαλύφθην

DEPONENT VERBS: MIDDLE/PASSIVE FORMS WITH ACTIVE MEANINGS
Many verbs lack active voice endings resulting in their middle/passive forms have active meanings. A few verbs have both active and middle/passive forms but with different meanings (e.g.: ἄρχω, "I rule"; ἄρχομαι, "I begin"). Here are some common deponent verbs in the NT:

COMMON NT DEPONENT VERBS

ἀπέρχομαι	"I go away"	ἐξέρχομαι	"I go out"
ἀποκρίνομαι	"I answer"	ἐργάζομαι	"I work"
ἀσπάζομαι	"I greet"	ἔρχομαι	"I come, go"
βούλομαι	"I wish"	εὐαγγελίζομαι	"I preach the gospel"
γίνομαι	"I become"	κάθημαι	"I sit"
δέομαι	"I pray"	πορεύομαι	"I go"
δέχομαι	"I receive"	προσέρχομαι	"I go to"
δύναμαι	"I can, am able"	προσεύχομαι	"I pray"
εἰσέρχομαι	"I come in"	χαρίζομαι	"I forgive"

εἰμί **CONJUGATION:** THE VERB "TO BE"
See the chart that follows.

εἰμί CONJUGATION: THE VERB "TO BE"

Indicative Mood

		PRESENT	IMPERFECT	FUTURE	PRESENT SUBJUNCTIVE	PRESENT IMPERATIVE	PRESENT OPTATIVE	FUTURE OPTATIVE
SINGULAR	1st	εἰμί	ἤμην	ἔσομαι	ὦ	—	εἴην	ἐσοίμην
	2nd	εἶ	ἦς	ἔσῃ	ᾖς	ἴσθι	εἴης	ἔσοιο
	3rd	ἐστί(ν)	ἦν	ἔσται	ᾖ	ἔστω	εἴη	ἔσοιτο
PLURAL	1st	ἐσμέν	ἦμεν	ἐσόμεθα	ὦμεν	—	εἴ(η)μεν	ἐσοίμεθα
	2nd	ἐστέ	ἦτε	ἔσεσθε	ἦτε	ἔστε	εἴ(η)τε	ἔσοισθε
	3rd	εἰσί(ν)	ἦσαν	ἔσονται	ὦσι(ν)	ἔστωσαν	εἴησαν	ἔσοιντο

PRESENT INFINITIVE: εἶναι

FUTURE INFINITIVE: ἔσεσθαι

Present Participle

The Present participle of εἰμί declines like the endings of ω verbs.

	SINGULAR			PLURAL		
	Masculine	Feminine	Neuter	Masculine	Feminine	Neuter
Nom.	ὤν	οὖσα	ὄν	ὄντες	οὖσαι	ὄντα
Gen.	ὄντος	οὔσης	ὄντος	ὄντων	οὐσῶν	ὄντων
Dat.	ὄντι	οὔσῃ	ὄντι	οὖσι(ν)	οὔσαις	οὖσι(ν)
Acc.	ὄντα	οὖσαν	ὄν	ὄντας	οὔσας	ὄντα

FUTURE PTC.	Masculine	Feminine	Neuter	Masculine	Feminine	Neuter
Nom.	ἐσόμενος	ἐσομένη	ἐσόμενον	ἐσόμενοι	ἐσόμεναι	ἐσόμενα

IRREGULAR VERBS: STEMS THAT RADICALLY CHANGE

Many verbs have irregular conjugation patterns with radical stem changes from one tense-form to another. Some of the irregular verbs most used in the NT are listed here in their six principal parts (base forms of compounds are given without reduplicating their cognates; e.g. ἔρχομαι is listed here but not εἰσέρχομαι, ἐξ-, προσ-, etc.). From these forms the rest of the conjugations can be projected. Those marked with a - are found only in compounds in the NT.

PRINCIPAL PARTS OF COMMON IRREGULAR VERBS

English Trans.	(1) PRESENT	(2) FUTURE	(3) AORIST-ACTIVE	(4) PERFECT	(5) PERFECT-M/P.	(6) AORIST-PASSIVE
"I lead"	ἄγω	ἄξω	ἤγαγον	—	-ῆγμαι	ἤχθην
"I hear"	ἀκούω	ἀκούσω	ἤκουσα	ἀκήκοα	—	ἠκούσθην
"I destroy"	ἀπόλλυμι	ἀπολέσω	ἀπώλεσα	ἀπόλωλα	—	—
"I forgive"	ἀφίημι	ἀφήσω	ἀφῆκα	—	ἀφέωμαι	ἀφέθην
"I go"	-βαίνω	-βήσομαι	-ἔβην	-βέβηκα	—	—
"I throw"	βάλλω	βαλῶ	ἔβαλον	βέβληκα	βέβλημαι	ἐβλήθην
"I become"	γίνομαι	γενήσομαι	ἐγενόμην	γέγονα	γεγένημαι	ἐγενήθην
"I know"	γινώσκω	γνώσομαι	ἔγνων	ἔγνωκα	ἔγνωσμαι	ἐγνώσθην
"I write"	γράφω	γράψω	ἔγραψα	γέγραφα	γέγραμμαι	ἐγράφην
"I receive"	δέχομαι	δέξομαι	ἐδεξάμην	—	δέδεγμαι	ἐδέχθην
"I am able"	δύναμαι	δυνήσομαι	—	—	—	ἠδυνήθην

COMMON IRREGULAR VERBS (Continued)

English Trans.	(1) Present	(2) Future	(3) Aorist-Active	(4) Perfect	(5) Perfect-M/P.	(6) Aorist-Passive
"I raise"	ἐγείρω	ἐγερῶ	ἤγειρα	—	ἐγήγερμαι	ἠγέρθην
"I come"	ἔρχομαι	ἐλεύσομαι	ἦλθον	ἐλήλυθα	—	—
"I eat"	ἐσθίω	φάγομαι	ἔφαγον	—	—	—
"I find"	εὑρίσκω	εὑρήσω	εὗρον	εὕρηκα	—	εὑρέθην
"I have"	ἔχω	ἕξω	ἔσχον	ἔσχηκα	—	—
"I desire"	θέλω	θελήσω	ἠθέλησα	—	—	—
"I die"	-θνῄσκω	-θανοῦμαι	-έθανον	τέθνηκα	—	—
"I stand"	ἵστημι	στήσω	ἔστησα	ἕστηκα	—	ἐστάθην
"I call"	καλέω	καλέσω	ἐκάλεσα	κέκληκα	κέκλημαι	ἐκλήθην
"I proclaim"	κηρύσσω	—	ἐκήρυξα	—	κεκήρυγμαι	ἐκηρύχθην
"I grasp"	κράζω	κράξω	ἔκραξα	κέκραγα	—	—
"I judge"	κρίνω	κρινῶ	ἔκρινα	κέκρικα	κέκριμαι	ἐκρίθην
"I take"	λαμβάνω	λήμψομαι	ἔλαβον	εἴληφα	-εἴλημμαι	-ἐλήμφθην
"I say"	λέγω	ἐρῶ	εἶπον	εἴρηκα	εἴρημαι	ἐρρέθην
"I see"	ὁράω	ὄψομαι	εἶδον	ἑώρακα	—	ὤφθην
"I persuade"	πείθω	πείσω	ἔπεισα	πέποιθα	πέπεισμαι	ἐπείσθην
"I drink"	πίνω	πίομαι	ἔπιον	πέπωκα	—	ἐπόθην
"I fall"	πίπτω	πεσοῦμαι	ἔπεσον	πέπτωκα	—	—
"I send"	-στέλλω	-στελῶ	-ἔστειλα	-ἔσταλκα	-ἔσταλμαι	-ἐστάλην
"I save"	σῳζω	σώσω	ἔσωσα	σέσωκα	σέσωσμαι	ἐσώθην
"I place"	τίθημι	θήσω	ἔθηκα	τέθεικα	τέθειμαι	ἐτέθην
"I carry"	φέρω	οἴσω	ἤνεγκα	ἐνήνοχα	—	ἠνέχθην

For the most complete listing of all NT verbs by principal parts, see Trenchard, *Complete Vocabulary Guide*, 237–72.

PART 2

GREEK SYNTAX SUMMARIES
With a Few Helps to Be Memorable

CASE USAGE GUIDE

INTRODUCTION: CASE NUANCES

The case ending is a function flag regarding the role a noun serves in its sentence, but these flags also have more nuanced signals. Prepositions help to clarify the use of a noun in a particular case (e.g., "*in* the house" vs. "*on* the house" vs. "*at* the house"), but a Greek author could use simple case endings without prepositions for such nuances as these. As always, context is the biggest help.

The listings below of uses for the Greek cases are not nuances of what the case spellings mean; rather, these are ways in which a case can be used. Further, a particular use of a case does not mean all of the case's nuance options should be read into that one occurrence. Some categories are overlapping and an author may well intend appropriate inclusiveness and word-play. But a reader should not assign to a particular case usage a significance the author has not intended.

The following are some of the primary case usage categories with definitions (and ***bold italicized*** key phrases), references to NT examples, and more extended examples where helpful. Most of the case usage definitions can be read with this introductory statement, "The case is used this way in contexts where it…"

VOCATIVE: THE CALLING CASE; *vocalizes* who is being addressed (e.g., Ἰατρέ in Luke 4:23; κύριε in 1 Cor. 7:16).

NOMINATIVE: THE NAMING CASE; typically *nominates* the subject.

1. Subject Nominative. Names the ***subject*** of a verb, the one performing the action (e.g., ὁ θεὸς in John 3:16).

2. Predicate Nominative. Names the "object" or "complement" of *an equative (a.k.a. copulative) verb* (e.g., θεός in John 1:1; ἔργα in Heb. 1:10).

3. Nominative in Simple Apposition. Simply *renames* the juxtaposed nominative noun (e.g., ὁ βαπτιστὴς in Matt. 3:1).

4. Nominative Absolute (a.k.a. Independent or Hanging Nominative). A nominative word or phrase *not used in a sentence*; occurs in exclamations (e.g., ἄνθρωπος in Rom. 7:24), greetings (e.g., Παῦλος … καὶ Σωσθένης in 1 Cor. 1:1), titles (e.g., Ἀποκάλυψις in Rev. 1:1), and proverbial statements with no finite verb (e.g., κύων and ὗς in 2 Peter 2:22).

5. Pendent Nominative. A nominative absolute that describes the topic in a sentence where *a pronoun represents* it (e.g., ὁ νικῶν for αὐτόν in Rev. 3:12; ὅσοι for αὐτοῖς in John 1:12).

6. Parenthetic Nominative. The subject of a *parenthetical* clause within a sentence (e.g., ὁ ἀναγινώσκων in Matt. 24:15).

7. Nominative for Vocative. Designates the *person(s) being addressed* (e.g., Σίμον in Matt. 16:17; ἡ παῖς in Luke 8:54).

8. Nominative of Appellation. The "object" of a *verb of naming* (e.g., ὁ διδάσκαλος καὶ ὁ κύριος in John 13:13; Ἀπολλύων in Rev. 9:11).

GENITIVE: THE MOST FLEXIBLE "OF" CASE; typically *generates* some description of the preceding (or head) noun.

1. Possessive Genitive. Shows possession or *belongingness* (e.g., τοῦ θεοῦ in Heb. 11:25); of persons in familial relationship, this is called a *Genitive of Relationship* (e.g., Ἰακώβου in Luke 24:10).

2. Genitive in Simple Apposition. Simply *renames* the head noun which is also in the genitive (e.g., τῆς μητρὸς in Matt. 2:11).

3. Epexegetical Genitive. Makes the idea of the head noun (whether genitive or not) *more specific*; "that is, —" or "which is —" (e.g., περιτομῆς in Rom. 4:11).

4. Partitive (or Wholative) Genitive. *Denotes the whole* of which the head noun denotes only a part (e.g., τῶν ὑπαρχόντων in Luke 19:8; τῶν ἁγίων in Rom. 15:26).

5. Attributive (or Hebrew) Genitive (a.k.a. Genitive of Quality). Functions as an *attributive adjective modifying the head noun*; "-like," "-ed," "-ful" (e.g., τὸ σῶμα τῆς ἁμαρτίας in Rom. 6:6, where "body of sin" = "sinful body").

6. Attributed (or Reversed) Genitive. Reversed so the head noun acts as the adjective *attributed to the genitive* (e.g., καινότητι ζωῆς in Rom. 6:4, where "newness of life" = "new life").

7. Material Genitive. Describes the material the head noun is *"made out of—"* (e.g., ῥάκους in Mark 2:21).

8. Content Genitive. Describes the contents of the head noun; *"full of—"* (e.g., τῶν ἰχθύων in John 21:8).

9. Genitive of Separation. Gives (often with a preposition) the *place "away from"* which the action of another noun or verb is done (e.g., τῶν ποδῶν in Matt. 10:14; ἁμαρτίας in 1 Peter 4:1).

10. Genitive of Source (or Origin). Gives (often with a preposition) the *source "from"* which the noun or action comes (e.g., τοῦ θεοῦ in Phil. 4:7; πατομῶν/λῃστῶν/γένους/ἐθνῶν in 2 Cor. 11:26).

11. Genitive of Comparison. *Completes a comparative adjective:* greater, less, etc., "than —" (e.g., τῆς τροφῆς in Matt. 6:25).

12. Subjective Genitive. The *subject of the head noun's verbal idea* (e.g., ἀγάπης τοῦ Χριστοῦ in Rom. 8:35, "Christ's love for us").

13. Objective Genitive. The *object of the head noun's verbal idea* (e.g., ἀγάπην τοῦ θεοῦ in Luke 11:42, "[your] love for God").

14. Genitive of Time. Shows the *time "during" which* the action takes place (e.g., τοῦ σαββάτου in Luke 18:12).

15. Spatial Genitive. Gives (often with a preposition) the physical *location* of the action (e.g., ὕδατος in Luke 16:24).

16. Genitive of Means/Agency. Denotes the *means "by"* which, or the *personal agent* "by" whom, something is done (e.g., σοφίας in 1 Cor. 2:13; θεοῦ in John 6:45).

17. Genitive of Reference/Association. Shows *"with reference to"* what the adjective or head noun pertains (e.g., λόγου in Heb. 5:13)

or the one whom the head noun (usually with a συν- prefix) is "in association with" (e.g.,τῶν ἁγίων in Eph. 2:19).

18. Genitive of Direct Object. The **direct object** of some particular verbs; e.g., note 5-senses verbs (*taste/eat of, smell of, touch/take hold of, hear of, see/perceive of*), emotive verbs (*desire, worry, accuse of*) and *fill of, remember/forget, rule*, and *share*.

19. Genitive Absolute. An **anarthrous genitive participle in a phrase with no other grammatical relation** to the rest of the sentence; the subject of the participle's action is also in the genitive (see also p. 78) (e.g., Καταβάντος δὲ αὐτοῦ… in Matt. 8:1).

20. Descriptive Genitive. Describes the head noun in a more ambiguous manner than all the above descriptors; *"is characterized by —"* (e.g., σωτηρίας in 2 Cor. 6:2).

DATIVE: THE CASE OF PERSONAL INTEREST; as in *dating*, typically names "to/for" whom an action is done.

1. Dative of Indirect Object. Names *"to"* whom the action is done (e.g., σοι in John 4:10; θεῷ in 2 Cor. 5:11); called *Dative of Recipient* if there is no verb (e.g., πᾶσιν τοῖς ἁγίοις in Phil. 1:1).

2. Dative in Simple Apposition. Simply **renames** the other noun in the dative case (e.g., τῷ σωτῆρί in Luke 1:47).

3. Dative of Interest (of Advantage or of Disadvantage). Has more intensified personal interest to the point of having a positive or negative effect on the indirect object (e.g., *"for—"* τῇ κοιλίᾳ in 1 Cor. 6:13; *"against—"* ἑαυτοῖς in Matt. 23:31).

4. Dative of Possession. Shows a noun is *"belonging to"* the dative noun (e.g., αὐτῷ in John 1:6; τινι ἀνθρώπῳ in Matt. 18:12).

5. Dative of Reference (or Respect). Shows the personal interest limiting the action *"(with reference) to"*(e.g., τῇ ἁμαρτίᾳ in Rom. 6:2); called *Ethical Dative* (*of Feeling*) when the dative is a person; "as far as—is concerned" (e.g., τῷ θεῷ in Acts 7:20).

6. Destination Dative. Gives the **destination or goal** "to" which the actor of an intransitive verb (i.e., with no direct object; esp. ἔρχομαι) is headed (e.g., τῇ οἰκίᾳ in Luke 15:25).

7. Locative Dative (of Sphere/Place). Defines the literal or figurative *location* of the action as "in—," "on—," or "at—" (e.g., τῷ πλοιαρίῳ in John 21:8; τῇ δεξιᾷ in Acts 2:33).

8. Dative of Time. Shows a *point of time "at/on" which* the action takes place, often with ἐν (e.g., τῇ τρίτῃ ἡμέρᾳ in Matt. 17:23).

9. Dative of Association. Indicates someone (or thing) *"with" whom* the action is accomplished (e.g., ἀπίστοις in 2 Cor. 6:14).

10. Instrumental Dative (of Means/Agency). **Indicates how** the action is performed, the means or tool "with" which it is done (e.g., ταῖς θριξὶν in John 11:2), or, rarely, **indicates who** (a personal agent) performs the action (e.g., αὐτῷ in Luke 23:15); called *Dative of Material* when the means is a substance not a tool (e.g., μύρῳ in John 11:2; δόξῃ καὶ τιμῇ in Heb. 2:7) .

11. Dative of Cause. **Indicates why** the action is performed; "on the basis of" or "because of" (e.g., τοῖς δεσμοῖς in Phil. 1:14).

12. Adverbial Dative (of Manner). **Indicates the manner** "in/with/by"which the action is performed; often "-ly" (e.g., παρρησίᾳ in John 7:26, "in boldness" = "boldly").

13. Dative of Direct Object. The direct object usually of very *person-oriented verbs* like *minister to (serve), give worship to, give thanks to, be (dis)obedient to, trust in (believe), follow.*

ACCUSATIVE: THE CASE OF EXTENT OR LIMITS ON THE VERB'S ACTION; makes *accusation* about what the subject did.

1. Accusative of Direct Object. **Receives the action of the verb** (e.g., τὸν κόσμον in John 3:16).

2. Double Accusative of Person-Thing. Gives **two separate objects** in the accusative: one personal and one impersonal (e.g., ὑμᾶς and πάντα in John 14:26, "he will teach *you* [person] *everything* [thing]"). With passive verbs, the person is subject and the thing is called an *accusative of retained object* (e.g., ἅς in 2 Thess. 2:15, "*what* you were taught").

3. Double Accusative of Object-Complement. Gives an accusative *object that is further described* by another accusative

term (e.g., τὸ ὕδωρ and οἶνον in John 4:46, "he made *water* [object] [into] *wine* [complement]").

4. Accusative in Simple Apposition. Simply *renames* the other noun in the accusative case (e.g., τὸν ἀδελφὸν in Mark 1:16).

5. Subject Accusative. The doer of the action of an *infinitive verb* (e.g., αὐτὸν with εἶναι in Luke 4:41).

6. Predicate Accusative. The predicate (substantive or adjective) describing a subject accusative with a *non-finite equative verb* (participle or infinitive); similar to predicate nominative constructions, which use finite equative verbs; (e.g., βλάσφημον with ὄντα in 1 Tim. 1:12–13; τὸν χριστὸν with εἶναι in Luke 4:41).

7. Pendent Accusative. A free-standing accusative word or phrase *represented by a pronoun* in the actual sentence (e.g., λίθον for οὗτος in Matt. 21:42).

8. Adverbial Accusative. *Qualifies the action* of the verb like an adverb, often to show manner, sometimes (esp. with prepositions) purpose, result, or cause (e.g., πρῶτον in Matt. 6:33; δωρεὰν in Matt. 10:8).

9. Accusative of Measure (or Extent). Marks the *temporal or physical extent of the action* (e.g., νύκτα καὶ ἡμέραν in Luke 2:37; ὁδόν in Luke 2:44).

10. Accusative of Reference (or Respect). Shows *"with reference to"* whom/what the action pertains (e.g., τὸν ἀριθμὸν in John 6:10).

Case and Time

- Genitive: *kind of time* (e.g., ἡμέρας, "during the day," Rev. 21:25)

- Dative: *point of time* (e.g., ἡμέρᾳ, "on the day" Luke 13:16)

- Accusative: *extent of time* (e.g., ἡμέραν, "for the day," Matt. 20:6)

  Oddly, there seems to be a rare Nominative for extent of time: ἡμέραι in Mark 8:2; Matt. 15:32; Luke 9:28.

Case and Agency

- With active verb, subject nominative as primary agent.

- With passive verb, ὑπό + genitive for primary agent.

- With passive verb, διά + genitive for intermediate agent.

- *Divine passive* when no expressed agent, but God is implied.

- With passive verb, rarely, the dative for primary agent.

  "All (subj. nom.) this happened in order that what was spoken by the Lord (ὑπὸ κυρίου) through the prophet (διὰ τοῦ προφήτου) might be fulfilled (divine passive)" (Matt. 1:22).

ARTICLE USAGE GUIDE

Greek has a definite article (ὁ, ἡ, τό, "the"), but no indefinite article ("a"). The Greek article's basic ability is to conceptualize things; that is, it can make any part of speech a noun (i.e., a concept). Its primary function is to identify, usually a thing the listener knows in some way. Semantically, with the article (articular), a noun is definite; without the article (anarthrous), a noun (θεός) can be indefinite ("a god"), definite ("the God"), or qualitative ("deity"). The article is used in a variety of situations.

1. Simple Identification. The article simply identifies a particular noun (e.g., τὸν κόσμον in John 3:16).

2. Anaphoric Article. To refer back to a previously mentioned (anarthrous) noun (e.g., τὰς δύο ἡμέρας in John 4:43; cf. v. 40).

3. Deictic Article. To point/refer to a substantive that is present to the speaker (e.g., ὁ ἄνθρωπος in John 19:5).

4. Par Excellence Article. Refers to a noun as the extreme example of its class (e.g., ὁ προφήτης in John 1:21; cf. Deut. 18:15).

5. Monadic Article. To refer to a noun that is truly unique, one-of-a-kind (e.g., ὁ ἥλιος and ἡ σελήνη in Mark 13:24).

6. Well-known (or Celebrity) Article. To refer to a noun that is well-known but has not been mentioned, is not an extreme example, nor one-of-a-kind (e.g., τῇ διασπορᾷ in James 1:1).

7. With Abstract Nouns. Abstract nouns in Greek often have an article, but not in English (e.g., ἡ σωτηρία in John 4:22).

8. Generic Article. To refer to a whole class and distinguish it from other groups (e.g., ὁ ἐργάτης in Luke 10:7).

9. As a Personal Pronoun. To take the place of the third person personal pronoun in the nominative case and only with μὲν … δέ or with δέ. (e.g., ὁ and ἡ in Matt. 15:26–27).

10. As a Possessive Pronoun. Introduces a thing clearly belonging to the contextual noun (e.g., τὰς γυναῖκας in Eph. 5:25).

11. With the force of a Relative Pronoun. Used in the attributive position when the modifier is not an adjective, but a genitive, a prepositional phrase, or a participle (e.g., Πάτερ ἡμῶν ὁ ἐν τοῖς οὐρανοῖς in Matt. 6:9).

12. Substantiver. To turn another part of speech into a noun, including adverbs (e.g., τοῦ νῦν in Acts 18:6), adjectives (e.g., οἱ πτωχοί in Luke 6:20), prepositional phrases (e.g., οἱ ἐκ περιτομῆς in Acts 11:2), infinitives (e.g., τὸ θέλειν and τὸ κατεργάζεσθαι in Rom. 7:18), participles (e.g., ὁ πιστεύων in John 3:16), particles (e.g., τὸ ναὶ in James 5:12), and whole clauses (e.g., τὸ [list of commands]… in Rom. 13:9).

13. Function Marker. To show adjectival positions (e.g., τὸν υἱὸν τὸν μονογενῆ in John 3:16), the case of indeclinable nouns (e.g., τοῦ Ἰσραήλ in Luke 1:68), and the subject nominative (esp. vs. predicate nominative, e.g., θεὸς ἦν ὁ λόγος in John 1:1).

Classic Article Rules

- *Colwell's Rule*: a predicate nominative that is definite usually lacks an article when it precedes the verb (e.g., σὺ βασιλεὺς εἶ τοῦ Ἰσραήλ in John 1:49, "you are the King [not "a king"] of Israel").

- *Granville Sharp Rule*: when a single article precedes two (or more) singular personal nouns (not names) joined by καί, the nouns refer to the same person (e.g., ὁ θεὸς καὶ πατὴρ in 1 Peter 1:3).

- *Apollonius' Canon*: in genitive phrases, usually the head noun and genitive are botharticular or both anarthrous (e.g., either ὁ λόγος τοῦ θεοῦ or λόγος θεοῦ, not ὁ λόγος θεοῦ or λόγος τοῦ θεοῦ).

- *Apollonius' Corollary*: in anarthrous genitive phrases, usually both nouns have the same semantic force of indefinite, definite, or qualitative (e.g., πνεῦμα θεοῦ in Matt. 3:16, "the Spirit of [the] God").

VERB USAGE GUIDE

TENSE-FORM: CONTEXT, NOT SPELLING, DETERMINES USE

English verb tenses have a time-based orientation (e.g., past/present/future time) and some other languages have a kind-of-action (German: *Aktionsart*) tense system (e.g., linear/punctiliar/completed kinds of action); both of these systems base tense-form selection on the historic action itself. Many Greek grammars in the last two hundred years have confusedly thought the same about the Greek language.

In NT Greek, however, tense-form selection is based primarily upon the way the author wishes to think about the action. This involves two considerations: 1) the *aspect* he chooses to focus on, and 2) the *spatial vantage point* he chooses to offer (see also "Introduction: Greek Verb Basics" in Part 1: Grammar above).

1. Aspect. An author can choose to look at a single action from one of three different aspects:

   - The progressive aspect (a.k.a. internal or imperfective aspect) views the action *as a process* (e.g., looking at a parade as it passes by) and is represented by the *Present* and *Imperfect* tense-forms.

- The summary aspect (a.k.a. external or perfective aspect) views the action *as a whole* (e.g., looking at a whole parade from a helicopter) and is represented by the *Aorist* and *Future* tense-forms. (Scholars debate the aspect of the future tense-form.)

- The stative aspect views the action *as a state* (e.g., being in the control room as parade coordinator looking at the state of the parade) and is represented by the *Perfect* and *Pluperfect* tense-forms. (Scholars debate whether these tense-forms belong to a stative aspect or to sub-categories of one of the other aspects.)

2. Spatial Vantage Point. An author can choose to look at an action from one of two different spatial vantage points:

- Proximity (as if up close or drawing nearer to the action).

- Remoteness (as if farther away from the action).

Despite the use of the word "spatial" here, the proximity/remoteness can be with respect to physical space, temporality, level of specificity, or level of attention in the narrative storyline.

Putting these two considerations together, we can compare/contrast Greek's six basic tenses-forms as follows:

Progressive (Imperfective) **Aspect**	Present	The action is being viewed as a *process* with some kind of nearness or *proximity*.
	Imperfect	The action is being viewed as a *process* with some kind of remoteness (usually temporal remoteness = in the past).
Summary (Perfective) **Aspect**	Future	The action is being viewed as a *whole* with some kind of *proximity* (usually temporal drawing near = in the future).
	Aorist	The action is being viewed as a *whole* with some kind of *remoteness* (often temporal remoteness = in the past).
Stative Aspect	Perfect	The action is being viewed as a *state* with some kind of nearness or *proximity*.
	Pluperfect	The action is being viewed as a *state* with some kind of *remoteness* (usually temporal remoteness = in the past).

So then, the other concerns related to the historic action itself (like time and kind-of-action) are portrayed by the Greek context and the lexical value of the term, *not* by the verb's spelling. The following categories represent various time and/or kind-of-action contextual settings in which the different tense-forms of the Greek verb can be used. NT examples using the verb ποιέω ("I do, make, produce") are provided where available for ease of comparing English renderings.

Present: The action is thought of as a *process* with proximity, in contexts of any kind of action and time.

1. Progressive (Descriptive) Present. In contexts of a *continuous action in progress* (e.g., ποιοῦσιν in Matt. 12:2, "your disciples *are [currently in the process of] doing* what is not lawful").

2. Instantaneous (Punctiliar) Present. In contexts where the action is *completed at the moment of speaking* (e.g., ποιῶ in Rev. 21:5, "Behold, I *[at this moment] am making* all things new").

3. Extending-from-Past (Durative) Present. In contexts of an *ongoing action from the past* into the present (e.g., δουλεύω in Luke 15:29,"*I have been serving* you for these many years").

4. Iterative Present. In contexts where the action occurs *repeatedly* (e.g., ποιοῦμαι in Rom. 1:9, "how unceasingly I *am [repeatedly] making* mention of you always in my prayers").

5. Customary (Habitual) Present. In contexts of a *habitual action* (e.g., ποιοῦσιν in Matt. 6:2, "as the hypocrites *are [habitually] doing*").

6. Gnomic Present. In contexts with a progressing view of the action as proverbial or a timeless, *universal truth* (e.g., ποιεῖ in Matt. 7:17, "every good tree *produces* good fruit…").

7. Historical (Dramatic) Present. In contexts where the action took place *in the past,* usually with verbs introducing discourse or with verbs of propulsion (Mark: 151x's; Matt.: 93x's; Luke: 11x's; Acts: 13x's) (e.g., λέγει in Matt. 8:4 and Mark 1:44, "And *he said [says]* to him…"; cp. Aorist in the parallel passage at Luke 5:14).

8. Culminative (Perfect) Present. In contexts where a past action has present *on-going results* (e.g., ποιεῖτε in Matt. 21:13, "you *are making [indeed, have made]* it a den of thieves"; cp. the Intensive Perfect in Mark 11:17).

9. Conative (Tendential, Volutative) Present. In contexts where the **action is attempted** (or about to be), but not yet done (e.g., ποιεῖς in John 13:27, "what *you are about to be doing*, do quickly").

10. Futuristic Present. In contexts where the action is **to take place in the future** (e.g., ποιῶ in Matt. 26:18, "I *will be [am] keeping* the Passover at your house with my disciples").

11. Present Retained in Indirect Discourse. Unlike English, Greek verbs in indirect discourse contexts (*reported speech/ thought/ perception*) retain the tense-form of their direct discourse (e.g., ποιεῖ in John 4:1, "the Pharisees heard that Jesus *was making…*").

IMPERFECT: The action is thought of as a **process with remoteness**, in contexts of any kind of action and time, but usually with temporal remoteness (i.e., in past time contexts).

1. Progressive (Descriptive) Imperfect. In contexts of a **continuous action in progress** (e.g., ἐποίει in John 5:16, "because he *was doing* these things on the Sabbath").

2. Ingressive (Inchoative, Inceptive) Imperfect. In contexts emphasizing the **beginning of an action** (e.g., ἐποιοῦντο in Acts 27:18, "on the next day, they *began putting* [things] overboard").

3. Iterative Imperfect. In contexts of a **repeated action in past time** (e.g., ἐποίει in Acts 16:18, "she *kept on doing* this for many days").

4. Customary (Habitual) Imperfect. In contexts of a **past habitual action** (e.g., ἐποίουν Luke 6:23, "for their fathers *used to be doing* likewise to the prophets").

5. Conative (Tendential, Volutative) Imperfect. In contexts where the **action was attempted** (or could be), but not yet done (e.g., ἐδίδουν in Mark 15:23, "And they *were trying to give* him wine mixed with myrrh, but he did not take it").

6. Imperfect Retained in Indirect Discourse. Unlike English, Greek verbs in indirect discourse contexts (*reported speech/ thought/perception*) retain the tense-form of their direct discourse (e.g., ἐποίει in Acts 9:39, "showing the coats and garments Dorcas *had been making* while she was with them").

Aorist: The action is thought of as a *whole with remoteness*, in contexts of any kind of action and time, but is often with temporal remoteness (i.e., in past time contexts).

1. Constative (Punctiliar, Global, Simple, Summary) Aorist. For a *past action unspecified* by the context as to its kind of action (e.g., ἐποίησεν in Luke 5:29, "And Levi *made* a great feast").

2. Ingressive (Inchoative, Inceptive) Aorist. In contexts that *emphasize the beginning of an action* (or some state) with its continuation unspecified (contra the Ingressive Imperfect) (e.g., ἐπτώχευσεν in 2 Cor. 8:9, "For your sake he *became poor*").

3. Culminative (Consummative, Effective) Aorist. In contexts where the action is *completed with continuing results* (e.g., ἐποίησεν in Matt. 13:28, "An enemy *has done* this").

4. Epistolary Aorist. In contexts where the action is *contemporary (or future) for a writer, but will be past for the reader* (e.g., ἔπεμψα in Col. 4:8, "I *sent [am sending]* him to you").

5. Proleptic (Futuristic) Aorist. In contexts where the action is *yet to take place* (usually after some condition) (e.g., ἥμαρτες in 1 Cor. 7:28, "If you do not marry, *you do not sin [will not have sinned]*").

6. Dramatic (Immediate-Past) Aorist. In contexts where the action has *just recently occurred* (e.g., ἐποίησεν in Matt. 26:13, "what she *has [just now] done* will also be told in memory of her").

7. Gnomic Aorist. In contexts with a summary view of the action as proverbial or a timeless, *universal truth stated more generically (remotely)* (e.g., ἐδικαιώθη in Luke 7:35, "And wisdom *is justified* by all her children").

Future: The action is thought of as a *whole with anticipatory proximity*, and thus almost always in future time contexts.

1. Predictive Future. In contexts where the action is *to take place in the future* (e.g., ποιήσει in John 14:12, "he *will do* greater things than these").

2. Imperatival Future. In contexts of *a commanded action* (e.g., ποιήσει in Heb. 8:5, "See, *you shall make* everything according to the pattern that was shown to you on the mountain").

3. Deliberative (Dubative) Future. In contexts of some uncertainty about the action, as in *questions* (e.g., ποιήσουσιν in 1 Cor. 15: 29, "What *will they do* who are being baptized for the dead?").

4. Gnomic Future. In contexts with a summary view of the action as proverbial or a timeless, *universal truth stated with more anticipation (proximity)* (e.g., ποιήσει in Mark 9:39, "For no one who *does [will do]* a mighty work in my name will be able soon afterward to curse me").

PERFECT: The action is thought of as a *state with (heightened) proximity*, in contexts of any kind of action and time.

1. Intensive (Resultative) Perfect. In contexts where the emphasis is on the *continuing results/effects* for a completed action (e.g., πεποιήκατε in Mark 11:17, "you *have made* it a den of thieves").

2. Extensive (Consummative) Perfect. In contexts where the emphasis is on the *completion of an action* (e.g., πεποίηκεν in Mark 5:19, "what great things the Lord *has done* for you").

3. Simple Perfect. For completed actions with continuing results/effects in contexts that combine *both Intensive and Extensive* ideas (e.g., πεποίηκεν in Mark 7:37, "He *has done* all things well").

4. Dramatic (Aoristic, Historical) Perfect. In contexts *absent of any notion of existing results* of the action (e.g., πεποίηκα in 2 Cor. 11:25, "a day and a night I *made it [was adrift]* at sea").

5. Present Perfect. For some verbs—particularly those with *stative lexical meanings* like ἵστημι ("I stand"), μιμνήσκομαι ("I remember"), οἶδα ("I know"), παρίστημι ("I am present"), and πείθω ("I am confident")—the Perfect is used like a Present (e.g., παρέστηκεν in Acts 4:10, "this one *stands* before you").

PLUPERFECT: The action is thought of as a *state with (heightened) remoteness*, in contexts of any kind of action usually with temporal remoteness (i.e., in past time contexts).

1. Intensive (Resultative) Pluperfect. In contexts where the emphasis is on the *results/effects that continued in the past* for a completed action (e.g., ᾠκοδόμητο in Luke 4:29, "the hill where their city *had been built [and was still]*").

2. Extensive (Consummative) Pluperfect. In contexts where the emphasis is on the *past completion of an action* more than on the continuing effects in the past (e.g., πεποιήκεισαν in Mark 15:7, "who *had commited* murder in the insurrection").

3. Past Pluperfect. For some verbs—particularly those with *stative lexical meanings* like εἴωθα ("I am accustomed"), ἴστημι ("I stand"), οἶδα ("I know"), παρίστημι ("I am present"), and πείθω ("I am confident")—the Pluperfect is used as a simple past tense (e.g., παρειστήκεισαν in Acts 1:10, "two men *stood*").

VOICE: VOICES WHO DOES AND/OR RECEIVES THE ACTION

The personal endings (see p. 26) portray the voice of the verb, i.e. the subject's relation to the verbal action: active—doing or causing the action, middle—both doing and receiving the action, passive—receiving the action. These voices are used in various contextual and lexical circumstances.

ACTIVE VOICE: The subject *activates* the action.

1. Simple Active. The subject *performs* the action (e.g., γινώσκει in Luke 16:15, "but God *knows* your hearts").

2. Causative Active. The subject *causes another* to do the action (e.g., ἐμαστίγωσεν in John 19:1, "*he* [Pilate] *scourged* [Jesus]").

3. Stative Active. The subject *exists* in the verb's indicated state (e.g., μακροθυμεῖ in 1 Cor. 13:4, "love *is patient*").

4. Reflexive Active. A *reflexive pronoun* shows the subject to act on himself/herself (e.g., σῶσον in Mark 15:30, "*save* yourself").

MIDDLE VOICE: The subject both *activates and receives* the action.

1. Direct (Reflexive) Middle. The subject *acts on himself/herself* (e.g., ἐνδυσάμενος in Acts 12:21, "Herod *clothed himself*").

2. Indirect Middle. The subject acts *for himself/herself* (e.g., ἐξελέξατο in Luke 10:42, "Mary *has chosen [for herself]* the good part").

3. Causative Middle. The subject *causes someone to act on/for himself/herself* (e.g., περιβαλεῖται in Rev. 3:5, "The one who conquers *will cause himself to be clothed* in white garments").

4. Permissive Middle. The subject *permits someone to act on/for himself/herself* (e.g., ἀπογράψασθαι in Luke 2:5, "Joseph went up from Galilee … [allowing himself] to be enrolled with Mary").

5. Deponent Middle. Some verbs have *middle forms with active meanings*; see page 49 above.

Passive Voice: The subject *receives* the action.

1. Simple Passive. The subject *receives* the action (e.g., βαπτισθήσεσθε in Acts 1:5, "you *will be baptized* with the Holy Spirit").

2. Permissive (Causative) Passive. The subject *permits* someone else to perform the action on him/her (e.g., πληροῦσθε in Eph. 5:18, "but [allow yourself to] be filled with the Spirit").

3. Deponent Passive. Some verbs have *passive forms with active meanings*; see page 49 above.

Mood: THE AUTHOR'S PORTRAYAL OF ACTUALITY

Mood describes the author's portrayal of the verbal action as an actuality (indicative), as a potentiality (subjunctive), as only a possibility (optative), or as an intention (imperative). This is the author's portrayal, not necessarily the situation in history. So, for example, just because information is asserted as true (in the indicative mood) does not mean it is true. Lies are spoken in the indicative mood—with the attitude/mood of actuality—so as to be more convincing! Rather than mood, some verb forms serve other functions: participles are verbal adjectives and infinitives are verbal nouns; each is covered in more detail below.

Indicative Mood: The action is *indicated* as if actual or real.

1. Declarative Indicative. To *assert that an action happens* or a condition exists (e.g., ἐξῆλθεν in Mark 4:3, "the sower *went out* to sow").

2. Interrogative Indicative. Used in *factual information* questions: what? and who?, not how? or whether? or where? (cp. Deliberative Subjunctive) (e.g., εἶ in John 1:19, "Who *are* you?").

3. Conditional Indicative. Used in the protasis of conditional sentences with εἰ *to assert the "if" clause* (e.g., ἔγνωσαν in 1 Cor. 2:8, "If *they had known*, they would not have crucified the Lord of glory").

4. Potential Indicative. Used with verbs of obligation, wish and desire (e.g., ὀφείλω, δεῖ, βούλομαι, θέλω) followed by an infinitive *to assert what would/could/or should be* (e.g., ὀφείλομεν in Acts 17:29, "We *ought* not to think that...").

5. Command Indicative. A future indicative can be used for a command (usually an OT quotation), see *Imperatival Future* (e.g., ἔσεσθε in 1 Peter 1:16, "*You shall be* holy").

῞Οτι Clauses in the Indicative Mood

- **Direct Discourse (Recitative) ῞Οτι:** ὅτι is not translated but is rendered by quotation marks (e.g., John 6:42, "How does he now say, 'I have come down from heaven'").

- **Indirect Discourse ῞Οτι:** "that," reporting what another said/perceived/knows without quoting it (e.g., Matt. 5:17, "Do not think *that* I have come to destroy the law or the prophets").

- **Appositional ῞Οτι:** "namely that," the ὅτι clause renames its antecedent (usually the word τοῦτο) in the main clause (e.g., Luke 10:20, "Do not rejoice in this, *namely that* the spirits are subject to you").

- **Epexegetical ῞Οτι:** "[to the effect] that," the ὅτι clause explains the antecedent, not merely renames it (e.g., Luke 8:25, "Who is this man *that* he commands the winds and the sea?").

- **Causal (Adverbial) ῞Οτι:** "because" (e.g., Matt. 5:3, "Blessed are the poor in spirit, *because* theirs is the kingdom of heaven").

SUBJUNCTIVE MOOD: An action is *submitted* as a probable potentiality.

1. Hortatory Subjunctive. The 1st person plural can be used to *exhort* others to join in some action (e.g., ἀποκτείνωμεν in Matt. 21:38, "Come, *let us kill* him").

2. Deliberative Subjunctive. Used in *behavior oriented* questions to ask how? or whether? or where?, and not for mere factual information on what? and who? (cp. *Interrogative Indicative*).

   a. Real Deliberative—asks about a possible solution to a real problem (e.g., ποιήσωμεν in Luke 3:10, "What *should we do?*").

   b. Rhetorical Deliberative—a question that serves as a thinly disguised assertion about a course of action (e.g., ἐπιμένωμεν in Rom. 6:1, "*Should we continue* in sin that grace may abound?").

3. Emphatic Negation Subjunctive. Used with the double negative οὐ μή *to emphasize negation* (e.g., οὐ μή εἰσέλθητε in Matt. 5:20, "*You will never [ever] enter* into the kingdom of heaven").

4. Prohibitive Subjunctive. μή + *Aorist subjunctive* can be used as a negative command (e.g., μή ... μεριμνήσητε in Matt. 6:34, "Therefore, *do not worry* about tomorrow").

5. Indirect Question Subjunctive. Used with an interrogative particle (τίς, ποῦ, etc.) in *a statement that reflects a (unstated) deliberative question* (e.g., που ... κλίνη in Luke 9:58, "The Son of Man has no place *where he could lay* his head").

6. Indefinite Subjunctive. A *generic or uncertain projection* about a person, place, or time.

   a. Indefinite Relative Clause—used after ὅστις or ὅς + ἄν = "whoever" (e.g., ὅς ... ἄν πίη in John 4:14, "*Whoever drinks* of the water that I will give him will never thirst again").

   b. Indefinite Local Clause—used with a local adverb like ὅπου + ἄν or ἐάν = "wherever" (e.g., ἐάν ἀπέρχῃ in Luke 9:57, "I will follow you *wherever you may go*").

   c. Indefinite Temporal Clause—used with a temporal adverb like ὅταν, ἐπάν, ἡνίκα for "whenever" or ἕως, ἄρχι, μέχρι[ς], ὡς ἄν for "until" (e.g., ὅταν ... ἀσθενῶ in 2 Cor. 12:10, "*Whenever I am weak*, then I am strong").

7. Potential Subjunctive. Used in a *subordinate clause*, often with a subordinating particle and projecting some contingency.

  a. Conditional—in the protasis of a future (3rd class) or universal (5th class) conditional sentence (ἐάν for "if") (see p. 81).

  b. Comparative—with ὡς ("like") or ὡς ἐάν ("as if") (e.g., ὡς … βάλῃ in Mark 4:26, "The kingdom of God is *like* a man who *scatters* seed on the ground").

  c. Concessive—with ἐάν ("even if, although") (e.g., ἐάν κρίνω in John 8:16, "*even if I should judge*, my judgment is true").

  d. ἵνα Clauses—the most common category of subjunctive use.

῞Ινα Clauses in the Subjunctive Mood

- **Purpose** ῞Ινα: "[in order] to" (can be ὅπως, μή, μήπως, μήποτε instead of ἵνα) (e.g., ἵνα σωθῶ in Acts 16:30, "What must I do *to be saved*?").

- **Result** ῞Ινα: "[with the result] that, so as to" (e.g., ἵνα πέσωσιν in Rom. 11:11, "They did not stumble *so as to fall*, did they?").

- **Substantival** ῞Ινα: the clause functions as a noun (subject, object, predicate nominative, or in apposition), "that" (e.g., ἵνα … ποιήσωσιν as object in Matt. 12:16, "He ordered them *that they should* not *make* him known").

- **Epexegetical** ῞Ινα: explains or clarifies the preceding noun or adjective, "that" (e.g., ἵνα … εἰσέλθῃς in Luke 7:6, "I am not worthy *that you should enter* under my roof").

- **Complementary** ῞Ινα: completes the thought of a helping verb like δύναμαι ("I am able"), θέλω ("I desire"), etc., "to, that" (e.g., ἵνα προφητεύητε in 1 Cor. 14:5, "I want you all to speak in tongues, but even more *that you prophesy*").

- **Imperatival** ῞Ινα: often after a verb of speech, the clause has the force of a command (e.g., ἵνα φοβῆται in Eph. 5:33, "and *let* the wife *respect* her husband").

OPTATIVE MOOD: The action is expressed as a possible *option*.

1. Optative of Wish (Voluntative Optative). Without ἄν, to indicate *a wish*; about 35x's in the NT (29x's in Paul) (e.g., πληθυνθείη in 2 Peter 1:2, "Grace and peace *be* yours *in abundance*").

2. Potential Optative. **With ἄν, to denote the possible consequence** (apodosis) of an omitted but inferable condition in a 4th class condition; 15x's in the NT (9x's in Luke; 6x's in Acts) (e.g., θέλοι in Luke 1:62, "What *he would like* to call it [if he could talk]").

3. Conditional Optative. **With εἰ, to denote a possible condition** (protasis) in a 4th class condition (e.g., πάσχοιτε in 1 Peter 3:14, "Even if *you might suffer* for righteousness, you're blessed").

4. Deliberative (Oblique) Optative. Involves an **indirect question** after an augmented verb (e.g., εἴη in Acts 21:33, "He inquired who *he might be*").

IMPERATIVE MOOD: The action expresses an intention or *imperative*.

1. Command Imperative. To depict a **positive command** (e.g., ἀγαπᾶτε in Matt. 5:44, "*Love* your enemies").

2. Prohibitive Imperative. Using μή (or a cognate) to depict a **negative command** or prohibition (e.g., μὴ φοβοῦ in Mark 5:36, "*Fear not*; only believe").
   Some take the negated Present imperative as a command to cease what has already been continuing and the negated Aorist subjunctive to prohibit its beginning, but this does always not hold true (e.g., Matt. 6:19–20). Others describe the negated Present imperative to be for more general prohibitions and the negated Aorist subjunctive to be for more specific prohibitions, but this too is not always the case (e.g., Matt. 8:9). Such kind-of-action concerns are gleaned from the context and lexical values, not the tense-form and mood spellings.

3. Request Imperative. To depict **requests**, encouragements, and prayer (e.g., δὸς in Matt. 6:11, "*Give* us today our daily bread").

4. Conditional Imperative. The command gives the condition for a future event (**imperative verb + καί + future indicative verb**) (e.g., αἰτεῖτε in Matt. 7:7, "*Ask* and it will be given").

Greek Commands Can Be Depicted By:
• The imperative mood (*Command* or *Prohibitive*).
• A future tense verb in the indicative—see *Imperatival Future*.
• A 1st person subjunctive—see *Hortatory Subjunctive*.
• μή + aorist subjunctive—see *Prohibitive Subjunctive*.
• ἵνα + subjunctive—see under *Potential Subjunctive*.
• An infinitive—see *Imperatival Infinitive*.
• A participle—see *Imperatival Participle*.
• Particular verbs with commanding lexical values in the indicative—see *Potential Indicative*.

INFINITIVES: THE NEUTER VERBAL NOUN

As a verb, an infinitive has tense and voice, can have a subject (always in the accusative case) and an object, and can be described by adverbs. As a noun, an infinitive is neuter in gender, can serve as a subject or object, can have an article and be in a particular case, and can be modified by adjectives and prepositions. Here are the primary uses of the infinitive, listed with *continuous enumeration but under three main categories*.

SUBSTANTIVAL INFINITIVES: Function predominantly as *nouns*.

1. Subject Infinitive. Functions as the *subject of a sentence* (e.g., κολλᾶσθαι and προσέρχεσθαι in Acts 10:28, "For a Jewish man *to associate* or *to visit* a foreigner is unlawful").

2. Direct Object Infinitive. Functions as *the complement/object* of a verb (e.g., τὸ ποιῆσαι in 2 Cor. 8:11, "but now also complete *the doing* [of it]").

3. Indirect Discourse Infinitive. The *direct object of a verb of speech, knowing, or perception* (e.g., εἶναι in Mark 12:18, "Sadducees ... who say *there is* no resurrection").

4. Appositional Infinitive. Simply **renames a prior noun**/pronoun (e.g., ἐπισκέπτεσθαι in James 1:27, "Pure and undefiled religion ... is this, *to watch over* orphans and widows").

5. Epexegetical Infinitive. Clarifies, explains, or **qualifies a noun** or adjective (e.g., τοῦ πατεῖν in Luke 10:19, "I have given you authority *to tread* on serpents and scorpions").

ADVERBIAL INFINITIVES: Function to **modify verbs**.

6. Temporal Infinitive. Helps express **the time of the main verb's action** by referencing the infinitive's action; with μετὰ τό ("after") for antecedent action, with ἐν τῷ ("while,") for contemporaneous action, with πρό τοῦ, πρίν, πρίν ἤ ("before") for subsequent action, and with ἕως τοῦ ("until") for just prior action (e.g., μετὰ τὸ ἀναστῆναι in Acts 10:41, "who ate and drank with him *after* he *arose* from the dead").

7. Purposive (Telic) Infinitive. Expresses **the purpose** for the main verb's action; used alone, with τοῦ, εἰς τό, πρὸς τό, ὡς, or ὥστε ("to," "in order to,") (e.g., ἀκοῦσαι in Acts 10:33, "we are gathered *in order to hear* all that was commanded").

8. Result Infinitive. Expresses **the (unintended) result** of the main verb's action; used alone, with τοῦ, εἰς τό, ἐν τῷ, ὡς, or ὥστε ("with the result that," "so that") (e.g., ὥστε βυθίζεσθαι in Luke 5:7, "they filled both boats *so that* they *began to sink*").

9. Causal Infinitive. Expresses **the cause or ground** of the main verb's action; with διὰ τό ("because") (e.g., διὰ τὸν ... ἔχειν in Matt. 13:6, "and *because they had* no root, they withered").

10. Complementary Infinitive. **Completes the thought** of a helping verb like δύναμαι ("I am able"), θέλω ("I desire"), etc., (e.g., γινώσκειν in Phil. 1:2, "I want you *to know* ...").

INDEPENDENT INFINITIVES: Function as an **independent** verb.

11. Imperatival Infinitive. **Functions as an imperative** verb (e.g., εἶναι in Titus 2:2, "*Let* the older man *be* sober").

12. Infinitive Absolute. Stands alone with **no grammatical relationship to the sentence**; usually in letter salutations (e.g., χαίρειν in Acts 23:26, "Claudius Lysias to the most excellent governor Felix, *greetings*").

PARTICIPLES: THE VERBAL ADJECTIVE

As a verb, a participle has tense and voice (not mood or person), can have a subject and an object, and can be described by adverbs. As an adjective, it is fully declineable into all three genders, must match any noun it modifies in gender-number-case, can serve to portray or modify a substantive, can have an article, and can be modified by adjectives and prepositions.

With adverbial participles, the relationship of its action to the main verb's action must be determined, particularly its time. This can be

- antecedent to the time of the main verb, which happens "after" the participle does;

- contemporaneous with the main verb, which happens "while" or "when" the participle does; or

- subsequent to the time of the main verb, which happens "before" the participle does.

The tense of a participle—following aspect theory and sensitive to context—usually is translated into English by the following guidelines:

- The Aorist tense generally views the participle's action as a whole and *antecedent* to the time of the main verb (or contemporaneous with an Aorist main verb).

- The Present tense generally views the participle's action as a process *contemporaneous* with the time of the main verb.

- The Future tense views the participle's action as whole and *subsequent* to the time of the main verb.

- The Perfect tense generally views the participle's action as a state *antecedent* to the time of the main verb.

The participle's primary contextual situations are listed below with *continuous enumeration but under four main categories.*

ADJECTIVAL PARTICIPLES: Function as *adjectives*.

1. Attributive (Dependent Adjectival) Participle. Used as an *attributive adjective* to modify an explicitly stated substantive and agrees with it in gender, number, and case; examples:

   a. 1st attributive [TAN]— ταῖς **συνελθούσαις** γυναιξίν in Acts 16:13, "the *gathered* women."

b. 2nd attributive [TNTA]— πόθεν οὖν ἔχεις τὸ ὕδωρ τὸ **ζῶν**; in John 4:11, "From where then do you have *the living water*?"

c. 3rd attributive [NTA]—Σίμων ὁ **λεγόμενος** Πέρτος in Matt. 10:2, "Simon *[the one] called* Peter."

d. 4th attributive [NA]—ἔδωκεν ἄν σοι ὕδωρ **ζῶν** in John 4:10, "he would have given to you *living* water."

2. Predicate (Dependent Adjectival) Participle. Used as a ***predicate adjective*** or as a predicate complement to modify a substantive and agrees with it in gender, number, and case; examples:

a. 1st predicate [ATN]—**Ζῶν** γὰρ ὁ λόγος τοῦ θεοῦ in Heb. 4:12, "For the word of God *[is] living*."

b. 2nd predicate [TNA]—θεωρῶ τοὺς οὐρανοὺς **διηνοιγμένους** in Acts 7:56, "I see the heavens *[are] opened*."

c. Complement with a copulative verb—**πρέπον** ἐστὶν ἡμῖν in Matt. 3:15, "it is *fitting* for us."

d. Complement in double accusative construction—παραστῆσαι τὰ σώματα ὑμῶν θυσίαν **ζῶσαν** ἁγίαν εὐάρεστον in Rom. 12:1, "present your bodies [as] a sacrifice–*alive*, holy, acceptable..."

3. Substantival (Independent Adjectival) Participle. The modified noun is missing and the participle ***assumes the noun's role*** (e.g., ἰώμενος πάντας τοὺς **καταδυναστευομένους** ὑπὸ τοῦ διαβόλου in Acts 10:38, "healing all *those being oppressed* by the devil").

4. (Pendant) Nominative Absolute Participle. A substantival participle that functions as a pendant nominative, i.e. the ***logical subject represented by a pronoun*** in the actual sentence (e.g., Ὁ **νικῶν** δώσω αὐτῷ καθίσαι μετ᾽ ἐμοῦ in Rev. 3:21, "*The one who conquers*, to him I will give to sit with me").

ADVERBIAL CIRCUMSTANTIAL PARTICIPLES: Function to ***modify main verbs***, somehow describing the main verb's circumstances.

5. Temporal Participle. While every adverbial participle has some temporal relationship with its main verb (see p. 75), the *temporal participle* expresses **only that time relationship** ("after," "while," "before") (e.g., **διερωτήσαντες** τὴν οἰκίαν τοῦ Σίμωνος ἐπέστησαν

ἐπὶ τὸν πυλῶνα in Acts 10:17, "*after asking directions* to Simon's house, they stood at the gate").

6. Instrumental Participle (of Means). Expresses the *means* by which the action of the main verb is accomplished ("by," "by means of") (e.g., καὶ φωνήσαντες ἐπυνθάνοντο in Acts 10:18, "And *[by] calling* out they asked").

7. Modal Participle (Instrumental Participle of Manner). Expresses the *manner* in which the action of the main verb is accomplished (usually a word of emotion or attitude) (e.g., Οἱ μὲν οὖν ἐπορεύοντο **χαίροντες** in Acts 5:41, "Therefore they went on their way *rejoicing*").

8. Purposive (Telic) Participle. Expresses the *purpose* of the action of the main verb ("to," "in order to," "for the purpose of") (e.g., ὃς ἐληλύθει **προσκυνήσων** εἰς Ἰερουσαλήμ in Acts 8:27, "Who had come *to worship* in Jerusalem").

9. Result Participle. Expresses the *(perhaps unintended) result* of the action of the main verb ("with the result of"); always a Present tense participle following the main verb (e.g., καὶ αὐτὸς ἐδίδασκεν ἐν ταῖς συναγωγαῖς αὐτῶν **δοξαζόμενος** ὑπὸ πάντων in Luke 4:15, "He taught in their synagogues, *[with the result of] being glorified* by all").

10. Causal Participle. Expresses the *cause or grounds* for the action of the main verb ("because," "since"); many times the English temporal translation is sufficient ("when" or "after") (e.g., ἀκούσας δὲ ὁ βασιλεὺς Ἡρῴδης ἐταράχθη in Matt. 2:3, "*Because* King Herod *heard* this, he was troubled").

11. Conditional Participle. Expresses the *protasis ("if")* for which the main verb is the apodosis ("then") (e.g., καιρῷ γὰρ ἰδίῳ θερίσομεν μὴ **ἐκλυόμενοι** in Gal. 6:9, "for in due time we will reap, *if we do* not *give up*").

12. Concessive Participle. Expresses *a concession*, implying that the state or action of the main verb is true in spite of the state or action of the participle ("even though," "although," "though") (e.g., τυφλὸς **ὢν** ἄρτι βλέπω in John. 9:25, "*although I was* blind, now I see").

13. Genitive Absolute Participle. An *anarthrous participle and a substantive, both in the genitive case*, that stand alone in a clause with no other grammatical relationship to the rest of the sentence,

usually at the front of the sentence and translated temporally (e.g., Ἔτι λαλοῦντος τοῦ Πέτρου τὰ ῥήματα ταῦτα ἐπέπεσεν τὸ πνεῦμα τὸ ἅγιον in Acts 10:44, "*While Peter was still speaking these words,* the Holy Spirit fell…").

ADVERBIAL NON-CIRCUMSTANTIAL PARTICIPLES: These somehow *accompany main verbs,* sometimes even completing them.

14. Participle of Attendant Circumstance. Expresses an action that *accompanied the action* of the main verb. While dependent upon (esp. the mood of) the main verb, it can be translated as additional circumstances added to the main verb's own ("and [participle as a finite verb]") (e.g., **συναντήσας** αὐτῷ ὁ Κορνήλιος **πεσὼν** ἐπὶ τοὺς πόδας προσεκύνησεν in Acts 10:25, "Cornelius *met* him *and, falling* at his feet, worshipped").

15. Participle of Indirect Discourse. An anarthrous participle in the *accusative case after a verb of speech, knowing, or perception* can function to portray indirect discourse (reported speech) (e.g., ἀκούσας δὲ ᾿Ιακὼβ **ὄντα** σιτία εἰς ῎Αιγυπτον in Acts 7:12, "when Jacob heard that *there was* grain in Egypt…").

16. Periphrastic Participle. Used as a *predicate complement* (thus, nominative) *of a verb of being* as a "roundabout" way of phrasing something (e.g., ὁ δὲ Κορνήλιος **ἦν προσδοκῶν** αὐτοὺς in Acts 10:24, "And Cornelius *was waiting* for them").

17. Redundant (Pleonastic) Participle. **(*Unnecessarily*) *repeats the idea of the main verb,*** usually with verbs of speaking (e.g., **ἀρξάμενος** δὲ Πέτρος ἐξετίθετο αὐτοῖς καθεξῆς **λέγων** in Acts 11:4, "And *beginning* Peter explained it to them in order *saying*").

18. Complementary Participle. Functions like a complementary infinitive *to complete the idea of the main verb* (e.g., σύ τε καλῶς ἐποίησας **παραγενόμενος** in Acts 10:33, "And you did well [were kind enough] *to come*").

INDEPENDENT VERBAL PARTICIPLES: Very rarely, some participles *behave independently from any verb* in the context.

19. Imperative Participle. The context makes clear that it functions *alone as an imperative* (if found with a finite imperative, like ἀναστὰς is with κατάβηθι καὶ πορεύου in Acts 10:20, it would

be considered a Participle of Attendant Circumstance) (e.g., **ἀποστυγοῦντες** τὸ πονηρόν, **κολλώμενοι** τῷ ἀγαθῷ in Rom. 12:9, "*be hating* the evil, *be cleaving* to the good").

20. Indicative Participle. Functions *like an indicative finite verb as the only verb* in a sentence (e.g., καὶ **ἔχων** ἐν τῇ δεξιᾷ χειρὶ αὐτοῦ ἀστέρας ἑπτὰ in Rev. 1:16, "and he *was having [or had]* in his right hand seven stars").

Note on Participle Use:

"It is often said that mastery of the syntax of participles is mastery of Greek syntax. Why are participles so difficult to grasp? The reason is threefold: (1) *usage*—the participle can be used as a noun, adjective, adverb, or verb (and in any mood!); (2) *word order*—the participle is often thrown to the end of the sentence or elsewhere to an equally inconvenient location; and (3) *locating the main verb*—sometimes it is verses away; sometimes it is only implied; and sometimes it is not even implied! In short, the participle is difficult to master because it is so versatile. But this very versatility makes it capable of a rich variety of nuances, as well as a rich variety of abuses."

—Daniel B. Wallace
Greek Grammar Beyond the Basics (p. 613).

Participle Usage Identification Guide

1. Parse the participle, then ask these questions in order until a label fits.
2. Does the participle have an article agreeing in gender, number, case (GNC)?
   YES: 3. Is it used to describe a substantive (must agree in GNC)?
      YES: *Attributive Participle.*
      NO: 4. Is it used as a noun *in a sentence?*
         YES: *Substantival Participle.*
         NO: *Nominative Absolute Participle.*
   NO: 3. Is it used directly with (not necessarily next to) a substantive?
      YES: 4. Are the participle and the noun (as its subject) in genitive case?
         YES: *Genitive Absolute Participle.*
         NO: *Attributive Participle.*
      NO: 4. Is it used directly with (not necessarily next to) a verb?
         YES: 5. Is it the predicate nominative of a copulative verb?
            YES: *Periphrastic Participle.*
            NO: 6. Is it in the nominative case?
               YES: 7. Adverbial Circumstantial Participle:
                   Go through the options on p. 76 asking how
                   it modifies the main verb (i.e., with regard to
                   time, means, manner, purpose, result, cause,
                   condition, or concession).
               NO: 7. Does it otherwise describe the main verb?
                  YES: 8. How?
                     SAME IDEA: *Redundant Participle.*
                     OTHER: *Ptc. of Attendant Circumstances.*
                  NO: 8. Does it work with a "helping" verb?
                     YES: *Complementary Participle.*
                     NO: 9. Is it accusative after a verb of speech,
                       knowing, or perception?
                       YES: *Indirect Discourse Participle.*
                       NO: Reconsider "YES: 7" above.
         NO: 5. Is it used independently from any other verb?
            YES: AS A COMMAND: *Imperatival Participle.*
                 AS THE ONLY VERB: *Indicative Participle.*
            NO: 6. Is it used as an anarthous noun?
               YES: *Substantive Participle.*
               NO: Reconsider "YES: 7" above.

CONDITIONAL SENTENCES

A conditional sentence is an "if–then" statement: a condition (protasis), if fulfilled, that is followed by some result (apodosis).

1. First Class (Real, Condition of Fact) Condition. The *protasis is asserted as true/fulfilled*, at least for the sake of the argument; is very common in the NT, about 300 times.

   - Form—if: εἰ + indicative of any tense (negative used: οὐ),
     then: any mood/tense.

   - Past Time: "if" with Aorist tense (e.g., **εἰ κακῶς ἐλάλησα, μαρ-τύρησον** περὶ τοῦ κακοῦ in John 18:23, "**If I spoke** in an evil way, [*then*] *testify* of the evil").

   - Present Time: "if" with Present tense (e.g., **εἴ** τις **λαλεῖ**, ὡς λόγια θεοῦ in 1 Peter 4:11, "**If** anyone **speaks**, [*then let him speak*] as one with words of God").

2. Second Class (Unreal, Contrary-to-Fact) Condition. The assertion of the *protasis is assumed to be unfulfilled*, at least for the sake of the argument; occurs about 50 times in the NT.

   - Form—if: εἰ + augmented indicative (negative used: μή),
     then: ἄν + augmented indicative.

   - Past Time: "if" with Aorist, Pluperfect, or Imperfect tense of εἰμί + "then" with Aorist or Pluperfect tense (e.g., **εἰ γὰρ ἔγνω-σαν**, οὐκ **ἄν** τὸν κύριον τῆς δόξης **ἐσταύρωσαν** in 1 Cor. 2:8, "For **if they had known**, *then they would* not *have crucified* the Lord of glory").

   - Present Time: "if" with Imperfect tense + "then" with Imperfect tense (e.g., **εἰ** γὰρ **ἐπιστεύετε** Μωϋσεῖ, **ἐπιστεύετε ἄν** ἐμοί in John 5:46, "For **if you believed** Moses, *then you would believe* me").

   - Exceptions: no ἄν in apodosis in Matt. 26:24; John 15:22, 24; Gal. 4:15, et al; mixed constructions in Luke 17:6 and John 8:39.

3. Third Class (Eventual, More-Probable Future) Condition. *Projects* that the fulfillment of the protasis in the [near] future will bring about the (eventual) *future fulfillment of the apodosis*; is very common in the NT, about 270 times.

- Form—if: ἐάν + subjunctive of any tense (negative used: μή),
    then: Future indicative or future idea.

- Future-oriented (e.g., **ἐὰν ἅψωμαι** κᾶν τῶν ἱματίων αὐτοῦ
  σωθήσομαι in Mark 5:28, "**If** only **I touch** his garments, *I will be
  healed*").

- Exceptions: εἰ + subjunctive in Luke 9:13; 1 Cor. 14:5; Phil. 3:12;
  and Rev. 11:5.

4. Fourth Class (Possible, Less Probable Future) Condition.
The protasis projects a supposition about the future and *suggests
less probability of fullment than 3rd Class*; is rare and only partial
in the NT.

  - Form—if: εἰ + optative of Present or Aorist tense,
      then: ἄν + optative of Present or Aorist tense.

  - Future-oriented (e.g., ἀλλ᾽ **εἰ** καὶ **πάσχοιτε** διὰ δικαιοσύνην,
    μακάριοι in 1 Peter 3:14, "But even **if you should suffer** because
    of righteousness, then [*you are*] blessed").

  - Note: only partial examples are found in the NT (mixed
    constructions, a verbless apodosis, missing the protasis or the
    apodosis, etc.): e.g., Luke 1:62; Acts 5:24; 8:31; 17:18, 27; 20:16;
    24:19; 27:12, 39; 1 Cor. 14:10; 15:37; 1 Peter 3:14, 17.

5. Fifth Class (Universal, Present General) Condition. Projects an
axiomatic thought with no element of futurity specified.

  - Form—if: ἐάν + subjunctive,
      then: indicative or imperative of any tense.

  - Proverbial in nature (e.g. καὶ **ἐὰν** βασιλεία ἐφ᾽ ἑαυτὴν **με-
    ρισθῇ,** οὐ **δύναται** σταθῆναι ἡ βασιλεία ἐκείνη in Mark 3:24, "**If**
    a kingdom **is divided** against itself, that kingdom *is* not *able* to
    stand").

PART 3

PHRASE DIAGRAMMING
With Enough Results to Be Motivating

DIAGRAMMING: A Brief Introduction

The goal of any kind of diagramming is always the same: to better grasp the author's flow of thought. Nevertheless, there are several different kinds of sentence diagramming and various adaptations of them (see the bibliography). We can outline four different kinds of sentence diagramming and distinguish between them as follows.

1. TECHNICAL DIAGRAMMING
In this type of diagramming *each word is syntactically tagged and specifically drawn* in relationship to the other words in the sentence. This complex approach results in spidery looking diagrams that rearrange the order of words to fit the roles they play in sentences.

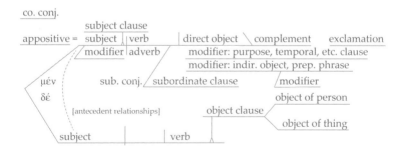

For more on this approach, see Thomas Schreiner, "Diagramming and Conducting a Grammatical Analysis," Chapter 5 in *Interpreting the Pauline Epistles* (2nd ed.; GNTE; Grand Rapids: Baker, 2011) 77–96.

2. Phrase Diagramming

Each phrase is drawn to illustrate its relationship to the other phrases and/or words in the sentence. Since it works with larger sections of the text, phrase diagramming is much less complex than technical diagramming. This approach goes by several other names including "phrasing" (Mounce), "block diagramming" (Kaiser), "making a sentence flow" (Fee), "developing a paragraph flow" (Easley), "grammatical diagramming" (Guthrie & Duvall), and even "textual transcription" (MacDonald). This is the basic approach we develop here.

3. Semantic Diagramming

Each phrase is syntactically tagged and drawn in relationship to the other phrases and sentences in the context in order to carefully trace the passage's argument. This approach enhances the simplicity of phrase diagramming with more technical, syntactical labeling. See Guthrie & Duvall move from phrase diagramming (pp. 23–37) to semantic diagramming (pp. 39–53) in *Biblical Greek Exegesis* (Grand Rapids: Zondervan, 1998).

4. Arcing

Without manipulating the words of the text, this method uses *a series of arcs* to group phrases together to visually represent the semantic relationships in the author's argument.

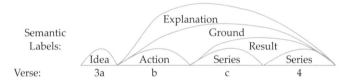

For more on this approach, see Schreiner, "Tracing the Argument," Chapter 6 in *Interpreting the Pauline Epistles*, 97–124, and esp. http://www.biblearc.com.

These approaches are not necessarily mutually exclusive, and an adaptation of *phrase diagramming* that incorporates some of the broader concerns of *semantic diagramming* is favored here.

THE BASICS OF PHRASE DIAGRAMMING

With the aim to be as practical as possible, as quickly as possible, at tracing the New Testament author's flow of thought, there are only a few basic underlying concepts to keep in mind.

1. MOTIVE

The use of phrase diagramming for outlining passages of Scripture requires the use of the original languages of Greek (for the New Testament) and Hebrew and Aramaic (for the Old Testament). Too often, those trained in these original languages find life in professional preaching and teaching careers or in lay teaching opportunities to be too busy to keep up their skills in working with these languages. The time demands of life and ministry are too much and the convenience of depending upon modern translations too tempting. The idea of taking valuable, fought-over time to diagram a sentence in the original language seems too much of a luxury and not time efficient enough to wedge into one's schedule.

But phrase diagramming is much *easier* than technical grammatical diagramming and much *clearer* in its structure and end product because the words that function most closely together are left together on one line. Consequently phrase diagramming is much *quicker* than technical diagramming and more *directly related* to creating a useful lesson/sermon outline. An hour (or less) of diagramming, will produce an outline by which to preach/teach a particular passage of Scripture.

2. GOAL

Phrase diagramming is certainly related to the study of grammar and syntax. The goal of phrase diagramming is to grasp the writer's general flow of thought and argument, which he has expressed in particular words and sentences. What the author means is to be found in what the author says and how he says it. Even as word studies are helpful to understanding the author's choice of terms, syntactical studies are important for understanding the author's argument. Phrase diagramming seeks to *picture the author's flow of thought.*

While many a pastor, Bible teacher, and preacher may often feel the pressure of getting another sermon or lesson prepared, the primary goal of this kind of diagramming—and any kind of sentence diagramming—is not simply to produce a good sermon or a good lesson. Rather, the primary goal is to discover the intended flow of thought or argument of the writer of Scripture. In doing this, the natural, secondary goal is for such a diagram to aid in the production of a fitting sermon/lesson outline, an outline that accurately represents the flow of the text for use in exegetical/expository (i.e., verse-by-verse) treatments of the text.

3. FOCUS

The verb is central to this diagram method. To ask, "What is happening in this text?" is to ask about the action expressed in it, which is generally embodied grammatically in the verb forms. That the *verbs are central* in phrase diagramming can be seen in that a series of arrows can usually be followed to a verb (or the verb's subject or object). Some arrows point from a noun to a verb to illustrate that noun as the verb's subject or object. Arrows from adverbs point to the verbs. An arrow from a temporal phrase will point to the verb it modifies. This focus on the verb does not mean that a sermon or lesson outline will always and only consist of verbs. Indeed, sometimes outlines will be made up of sub-points whose titles are nouns. But even for such lessons, each sub-point will likely be explained with some verbal idea found in the text.

4. Principles

Phrase diagramming is kept on track by three main principles. William Mounce—in *A Graded Reader of Biblical Greek* (Grand Rapids: Zondervan, 1996), xv—gives the three basic principles as follows:

- The more dominant phrases are further to the left on the page.

- Subordinate ideas are indented, placed under (or over) the concept to which they are related.

- Parallel ideas are indented the same distance from the left.

A few other principles will be explained in the next few pages, but these three govern the whole of phrase diagramming.

5. Flexibility

Most diagram instructors recognize a need for flexibility in diagramming to meet the personal needs of individual exegetes. A less technical approach to diagramming grants the user greater freedoms. While the operative question in more technical grammatical diagramming may be, What is the exact relationship of this word to the rest of the sentence? the freeing question in phrase diagramming is, *How can I diagram the phrases of this paragraph so that its structure is more visible to me?*

Of course, clearly it is possible to incorrectly diagram a passage, missing the author's intended meaning. In fact, going through the process of phrase diagramming may sometimes force the exegete to modify his/her prior exegetical conclusions about a passage. Flexibility is never to overshadow discovery of the author's meaning. Rather, the process of phrase diagramming will quickly get the exegete to ask the correct questions about the meaning of the text because he/she is struggling with the structure of the text. So then, within the limits of the author's intended meaning, the flexibility of phrase diagramming allows two interpreters to draw their diagrams of a text differently but still have the same interpretation of the passage's meaning.

STEP-BY-STEP PHRASE DIAGRAMMING

Part of the flexibility of phrase diagramming comes into play when discussing the number (and order) of steps to actually constructing a phrase diagram. The following eight steps are suggested in what seems to be a natural order. The text of 1 Peter 1:3–9 is used as an example.

1. ESTABLISH THE LIMITS OF THE PARAGRAPH

It is always helpful to read the entire book through quickly in English to get a broad overview of the writer's message or argument and the various parts and paragraphs of that message or argument. Of course, after diagramming a section of Scripture, you may find it desirable to adjust your initial assumptions regarding the extent of a particular passage and so adjust your paragraph breaks. Remember, the chapter and verse numbers in the Bible were added just a few hundred years ago for ease of referencing and are not part of the inspired text. Don't be fooled by the placement of chapter, verse, and paragraph breaks in the English translation. Watch for the author's flow of thought.

Step 1 Example

The critical Greek texts of 1 Peter 1:3–9 —the United Bible Societies' *Greek New Testament*, 4th rev. ed. (UBS⁴), the Nestle-Aland *Novum Testamentum Graece*, 28th ed. (NA²⁸), and SBL's *The Greek New Testament* (SBLGNT)—indicate this to be a paragraph made up of three Greek sentences (vv. 3–5, vv. 6–7, and vv. 8–9). A cursory reading of English translations shows that translators agree that this is a paragraph unit.

Step 1 (Paragraph Identification): 1 Peter 1:3–9

3 Εὐλογητὸς ὁ θεὸς καὶ πατὴρ τοῦ κυρίου ἡμῶν Ἰησοῦ Χριστοῦ, ὁ κατὰ τὸ πολὺ αὐτοῦ ἔλεος ἀναγεννήσας ἡμᾶς εἰς ἐλπίδα ζῶσαν δι' ἀναστάσεως Ἰησοῦ Χριστοῦ ἐκ νεκρῶν, 4 εἰς κληρονομίαν ἄφθαρτον καὶ ἀμίαντον καὶ ἀμάραντον, τετηρημένην ἐν οὐρανοῖς εἰς ὑμᾶς 5 τοὺς ἐν δυνάμει θεοῦ φρουρουμένους διὰ πίστεως εἰς σωτηρίαν ἑτοίμην ἀποκαλυφθῆναι ἐν καιρῷ ἐσχάτῳ. 6 ἐν ᾧ ἀγαλλιᾶσθε, ὀλίγον ἄρτι εἰ δέον [ἐστὶν] λυπηθέντες ἐν ποικίλοις πειρασμοῖς, 7 ἵνα τὸ δοκίμιον ὑμῶν τῆς πίστεως πολυτιμότερον χρυσίου τοῦ ἀπολλυμένου διὰ πυρὸς δὲ δοκιμαζομένου, εὑρεθῇ εἰς ἔπαινον καὶ δόξαν καὶ τιμὴν ἐν ἀποκαλύψει Ἰησοῦ Χριστοῦ. 8 ὃν οὐκ ἰδόντες ἀγαπᾶτε, εἰς ὃν ἄρτι μὴ ὁρῶντες πιστεύοντες δὲ ἀγαλλιᾶσθε χαρᾷ ἀνεκλαλήτῳ καὶ δεδοξασμένῃ, 9 κομιζόμενοι τὸ τέλος τῆς πίστεως [ὑμῶν] σωτηρίαν ψυχῶν.

2. Divide the Sentences into Their Natural Phrases

More correctly speaking, a *phrase* is a syntactically functioning group of words without a verb and a *clause* is a syntactically functioning group of words with a verb. The very title of this discipline actually uses the term *phrase* in a broader sense that encompasses both clauses and verbless phrases. When dividing a passage into its separate phrases, they should be kept in order as much as possible and each phrase and clause should be placed on a new line. In accomplishing this task using a word processor, steps 2–5 can be done separately. If one is creating a diagram with pencil and paper, steps 2–5 should be accomplished simultaneously so as to minimize erasures!

The punctuation marks of the UBS[4], NA[28] and SBLGNT can be helpful in determining phrase and clause breaks as can noting words that typically begin a phrase or clause. The following list of terms is reworked from Kendell Easley, *User-Friendly Greek* (Nashville: B & H, 1994), 21–23, 31. Remember, however, that some of these terms are postpositives (e.g., γάρ, δέ, μέν, οὖν, τέ, τίς/τί, and χωρίς) and will not be the first word in their particular phrases or clauses; nevertheless, postpositives are still a sign that the beginning of a new phrase or clause is just a word or two earlier.

Proper Prepositions—begin prepositional phrases (see p. 22) (altered before words with an initial vowel): ἀνά (ἀν᾽), ἀντί (ἀντ᾽, ἀνθ᾽), ἀπό (ἀπ᾽, ἀφ᾽), διά (δι᾽), εἰς, ἐκ (ἐξ), ἐν, ἐπι, (ἐπ᾽, ἐφ᾽), κατά (κατ᾽, καθ᾽), μετά (μετ᾽, μεθ᾽), παρά (παρ᾽), περί, πρό, προς, σύν, ὑπέρ, and ὑπό (ὑπ᾽, ὑφ᾽).

Improper Prepositions—are adverbs sometimes used as prepositions (see p. 23): e.g., ἅμα, ἄχρι, ἐγγύς, ἔμπροσθεν, ἕνεκα, ἐνώπιον, ἔξω, ἔξωθεν, ἐπάνω, ἕως, μέσος (-η, -ον), μέχρι, ὀπίσω, πέραν, πλήν, πλησίον, ὑποκάτω, χωρίς.

Relative Pronouns—begin relative clauses: ὅς, ἥ, ὅ (and its declension) and ὅστις, ἥτις, ὅτι (and its declension).

Coordinating Conjunctions—sometimes used to join two clauses (but also used to join two concepts within a phrase or clause):

Continuation	καί, δέ, τε ("and")
Disjunction	ἤ, εἴτε ("or")
Inference	οὖν, δίο, ἄρα ("therefore")
Cause	γάρ ("for, because")
Negative	οὐδέ, οὔτε, μηδέ, μήτε ("and not, not")
Adversative	ἀλλά, δέ, μὲν...δέ ("but") πλήν, μέντοι, καίτοι ("however")

Subordinate Conjunctions—used to join dependent clauses to a main clause:

Purpose	ἵνα, ὅπως ("in order to, that") μὴ πως, μήποτε ("in order not to")
Result	ἵνα, ὥστε (so that)
Cause	ὅτι, διότι, ἐπεί, ὡς ("because")
Condition	εἰ, ἐάν, εἴπερ, ἄν ("if")
Concession	εἰ καί, ἐάν καί, κἄν ("even if, although")
Comparison	καθώς, ὥσπερ, ὡς ("as, just as") ὡς ἐάν ("as if")
Place	ὅπου, οὗ ("where")
Time	ὅτε, ὡς ("when") ὅταν, ὡς ἄν ("whenever") local adverb + ἄν or ἐάν ("whenever") ἕως, ἄρχι, μεχρι(ς), ὡς ἄν ("until")
Discourse	ὅτι ("that" for indirect, "..." for direct)

Another helpful thing to remember is that finite verb forms usually function in separate clauses. While non-finite verb forms (participles and infinitives) sometimes function as substantives (the subject, object, or complement) in the same clause as a finite verb, sometimes they function in separate adjectival or adverbial clauses describing a substantive or the verb in the main clause.

Step 2 Example

The following sketch shows the phrases/clauses of 1 Peter 1:3–9 on separate lines. For problematic issues like the embedded phrase at 1 Peter 1:5 (τοὺς **ἐν δυνάμει θεοῦ φρουρουμένους**), see the section on Special & Problem Issues below.

Steps 2 & 3 (Phrases & Main Clauses) for 1 Peter 1:3–9

*3 Εὐλογητὸς ὁ θεὸς καὶ πατὴρ τοῦ κυρίου ἡμῶν Ἰησοῦ Χριστοῦ,
ὁ κατὰ τὸ πολὺ αὐτοῦ ἔλεος ἀναγεννήσας ἡμᾶς
εἰς ἐλπίδα ζῶσαν
δι᾽ ἀναστάσεως Ἰησοῦ Χριστοῦ
ἐκ νεκρῶν,

4 εἰς κληρονομίαν ἄφθαρτον
καὶ ἀμίαντον
καὶ ἀμάραντον,
τετηρημένην
ἐν οὐρανοῖς
εἰς ὑμᾶς

5 τοὺς ἐν δυνάμει θεοῦ φρουρουμένους
διὰ πίστεως
εἰς σωτηρίαν
ἑτοίμην ἀποκαλυφθῆναι
ἐν καιρῷ ἐσχάτῳ.

6 ἐν ᾧ
* ἀγαλλιᾶσθε,
ὀλίγον ἄρτι
εἰ δέον [ἐστὶν] λυπηθέντες
ἐν ποικίλοις πειρασμοῖς

7 ἵνα τὸ δοκίμιον ὑμῶν τῆς πίστεως
πολυτιμότερον χρυσίου
τοῦ ἀπολλυμένου διὰ πυρὸς δὲ δοκιμαζομένου,
εὑρεθῇ
εἰς ἔπαινον καὶ δόξαν καὶ τιμὴν
ἐν ἀποκαλύψει Ἰησοῦ Χριστοῦ.

8 ὃν οὐκ ἰδόντες ἀγαπᾶτε,
εἰς ὃν ἄρτι μὴ ὁρῶντες πιστεύοντες
δὲ ἀγαλλιᾶσθε χαρᾷ ἀνεκλαλήτῳ καὶ δεδοξασμένῃ,

9 κομιζόμενοι τὸ τέλος τῆς πίστεως [ὑμῶν]
σωτηρίαν ψυχῶν

3. IDENTIFY THE MAIN CLAUSES OF THE PARAGRAPH

Main clauses will likely each have a finite verb form in the indicative or imperative mood. These clauses remain out-dented furthest to the left in the diagram. Remember, however, that not all finite verbs are main verbs, since subordinate clauses can have finite verbs as well (e.g., the whole sentence of 1 Peter 1:8–9 has a finite verb, but it is subordinate to the sentence of vv. 6–7). Remember, too, that compound sentences may have more than one main clause—and, thus, have more than one main verb—and will be drawn on two parallel lines equally out-dented to the left.

Step 3 Example

The two main clauses of 1 Peter 1:3–9 have been identified in the Step 2 diagram above with an asterisk (*) in the far left margin, one in v. 3 and the other in v. 6.

---

4. INDENT THE SUBORDINATE PHRASES AND CLAUSES

In this step, every phrase (in the more technical sense—i.e., a word grouping *without* a verb) is considered subordinate to the noun or verb it modifies. This is also true of subordinate clauses. Each subordinate phrase and clause should be indented until it is directly below (or above) the part of the main clause (or other clause or phrase) that it modifies.

A subordinate clause (*clause* in the more technical sense—i.e., a word grouping *with* a verb) can be identified in several different ways. A clause is likely to be subordinate (but not necessarily) if it has one or more of the following features:

- if it begins with a subordinate conjunction (see list on p. 89),

- if it begins with a relative pronoun,

- if its controlling verb is in the subjunctive mood, or

- if its controlling verb is an infinitive or a participle.

Again, remember that subordinate clauses can have finite verbs.

Step 4 Example

In the indenting illustrated here, note that problematic features in 1 Peter 1:3–9 have been treated as per Special & Problem Issues below (e.g., the inserted ellipses).

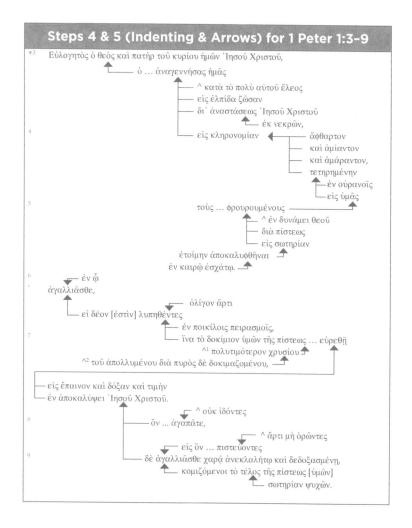

5. Draw Arrows from Each Subordinate Phrase

Arrows should be drawn from each subordinate item to the feature in the ruling phrase or clause that it modifies. Drawing arrows in the diagram will help clarify the indentation of subordinate phrases. Typically a string of arrows can be followed to the primary components of the main clause: the subject, the main verb, or the object. Different word processing programs offer different means of drawing arrows.

Step 5 Example

Arrows pointing from subordinate phrases in 1 Peter 1:3–9 to the features they modify are drawn in the diagram on page 92.

6. ADD SEMANTIC LABELS

At this point, the exegete can incorporate selective features of semantic diagramming. A key question to ask constantly while phrase diagramming is, "*How* is this phrase related the feature it modifies?" Answers to this question can be added to the diagram in single-word semantic labels inside brackets. Easley (*User-Friendly Greek*, 25–26) says that a main clause can typically be labeled as one of three kinds: introductory sentence, development sentence, or summary sentence. Similarly, each subordinate clause functions in only one of three basic ways: as a substantive (standing in for a noun), as an adjective (modifying a noun, pronoun, or substantive), or as an adverb (modifying a verb). Despite this appropriate simplicity, more complexity may be helpful. There are, for example, different kinds of adjectives (e.g., color, size, weight, attitude) and different kinds of adverbs (e.g., manner, time, location, purpose, result). Some may find help in remembering the basic questions of Who? What? When? Where? Why? and How?, for a subordinate phrase or clause typically answers one of these simple questions in relation to its ruling clause.

More technical lists of syntactical relationship descriptors are suggested by some scholars. Guthrie and Duvall give a far more detailed taxonomy of semantic function labels with explanations and New Testament examples (*Biblical Greek Exegesis*, 43–52). Wrestling with the precise distinction between some of the various categories is sometimes difficult as applied to a particular passage (e.g., "purpose" vs. "result"), but not unimportant. Regarding this step, Guthrie and Duvall write, "We have found it to be the single most dynamic tool to move a student from the nuts and bolts of grammar toward a comprehension of a whole passage's structure and message. Such comprehension stands prerequisite to an accurate teaching or preaching of the text." An adaptation of Guthrie and Duvall's list of labels appears on page 96 below.

Adopting a particular scholar's list of descriptors is not as important as using descriptors that will help the individual exegete properly trace the flow of the author's argument.

Steps 6 & 7 Examples

On page 94 is the diagram of 1 Peter 1:3–9 with application of semantic labels, both simple labels and some from Guthrie and Duvall, as per Step 6. On page 95 is the same diagram of 1 Peter 1:3–9 with the NIV translation, as per Step 7.

Step 6 (Semantic Labels) for 1 Peter 1:3–9

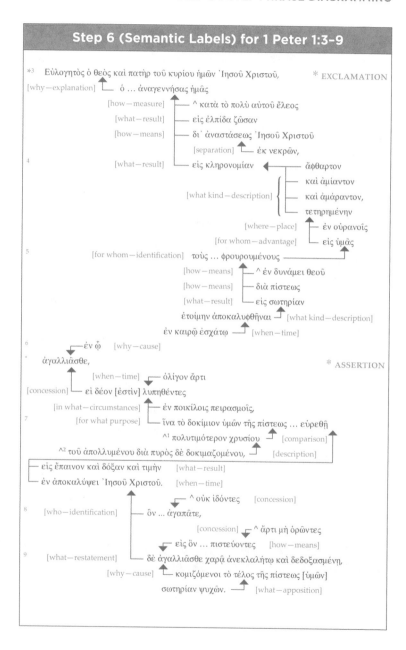

*3 Εὐλογητὸς ὁ θεὸς καὶ πατὴρ τοῦ κυρίου ἡμῶν Ἰησοῦ Χριστοῦ,   * EXCLAMATION

[why—explanation]   ὁ … ἀναγεννήσας ἡμᾶς

       [how—measure]   ^ κατὰ τὸ πολὺ αὐτοῦ ἔλεος

       [what—result]   εἰς ἐλπίδα ζῶσαν

       [how—means]   δι᾽ ἀναστάσεως Ἰησοῦ Χριστοῦ

          [separation]   ἐκ νεκρῶν,

4   [what—result]   εἰς κληρονομίαν ◄   ἄφθαρτον

                                               καὶ ἀμίαντον

       [what kind—description]   καὶ ἀμάραντον,

                                              τετηρημένην

          [where—place]   ἐν οὐρανοῖς

          [for whom—advantage]   εἰς ὑμᾶς

5   [for whom—identification]   τοὺς … φρουρουμένους

       [how—means]   ^ ἐν δυνάμει θεοῦ

       [how—means]   διὰ πίστεως

       [what—result]   εἰς σωτηρίαν

         ἑτοίμην ἀποκαλυφθῆναι   [what kind—description]

         ἐν καιρῷ ἐσχάτῳ   [when—time]

6   ἐν ᾧ   [why—cause]

    ἀγαλλιᾶσθε,   * ASSERTION

         [when—time]   ὀλίγον ἄρτι

[concession]   εἰ δέον [ἐστὶν] λυπηθέντες

     [in what—circumstances]   ἐν ποικίλοις πειρασμοῖς,

7   [for what purpose]   ἵνα τὸ δοκίμιον ὑμῶν τῆς πίστεως … εὑρεθῇ

         ^1 πολυτιμότερον χρυσίου   [comparison]

     ^2 τοῦ ἀπολλυμένου διὰ πυρὸς δὲ δοκιμαζομένου,   [description]

  εἰς ἔπαινον καὶ δόξαν καὶ τιμὴν   [what—result]

  ἐν ἀποκαλύψει Ἰησοῦ Χριστοῦ.   [when—time]

          ^ οὐκ ἰδόντες   [concession]

8   [who—identification]   ὃν … ἀγαπᾶτε,

         [concession]   ^ ἄρτι μὴ ὁρῶντες

        εἰς ὃν … πιστεύοντες   [how—means]

9   [what—restatement]   δὲ ἀγαλλιᾶσθε χαρᾷ ἀνεκλαλήτῳ καὶ δεδοξασμένῃ,

       [why—cause]   κομιζόμενοι τὸ τέλος τῆς πίστεως [ὑμῶν]

       σωτηρίαν ψυχῶν.   [what—apposition]

Step 7 (English Diagram) for 1 Peter 1:3–9

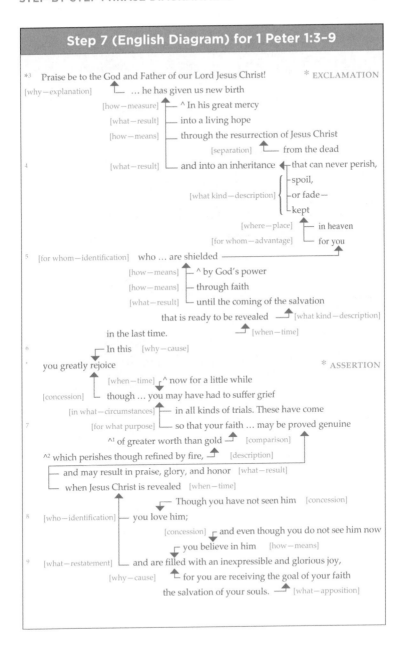

*3 Praise be to the God and Father of our Lord Jesus Christ!   * EXCLAMATION

[why—explanation]   └─ … he has given us new birth

          [how—measure] ┌─ ^ In his great mercy

            [what—result] ├── into a living hope

            [how—means] ├── through the resurrection of Jesus Christ

               [separation] └── from the dead

4   [what—result] └── and into an inheritance ◄─ that can never perish,

                                              ┌─ spoil,

        [what kind—description] { ├─ or fade—

                                        └─ kept

               [where—place] ┌── in heaven

           [for whom—advantage] └── for you

5 [for whom—identification] who … are shielded ─────────────────

          [how—means] ┌─ ^ by God's power

          [how—means] ├─ through faith

        [what—result] └─ until the coming of the salvation

            that is ready to be revealed ─┐ [what kind—description]

           in the last time. ─┐ [when—time]

6   ┌─ In this   [why—cause]

   you greatly rejoice   * ASSERTION

          [when—time] ┌─ ^ now for a little while

[concession] └─ though … you may have had to suffer grief

     [in what—circumstances] ┌── in all kinds of trials. These have come

       [for what purpose] └── so that your faith … may be proved genuine

7   ^1 of greater worth than gold ─┐ [comparison]

^2 which perishes though refined by fire, ─┐ [description]

 ┌─ and may result in praise, glory, and honor [what—result]

 └─ when Jesus Christ is revealed [when—time]

                    ┌─ Though you have not seen him [concession]

8 [who—identification] ├─ you love him;

              [concession] ┌─ and even though you do not see him now

                    ┌─ you believe in him [how—means]

9 [what—restatement] └─ and are filled with an inexpressible and glorious joy,

       [why—cause] └─ for you are receiving the goal of your faith

          the salvation of your souls. ─┐ [what—apposition]

Semantic Labels for Diagramming		
BASIC EXPRESSIONS	**EVENTS/ACTIONS**	**ARGUMENT/DISCUSSION**
Assertion	*Temporal Labels:*	*Logic Labels:*
Event or Action	Time	Basis
Rhetorical Question	Simultaneous	Inference
Desire (wish or hope)	Sequence	Condition
Exclamation	Progression	Concession
Exhortation (command	*Local Labels:*	Contrast or Compare
or encouragement)	Place	General or Specific
Warning	Sphere	*Clarification Labels:*
Promise	Source	Restatement
Problem/Resolution	Separation	Description
Entreaty	*Other Labels:*	Identification
	Measure	Illustration/Example
	Circumstance	Apposition
	Object (dir./ind.)	Explanation
	Cause	Expansion
	Result	Alternative
	Purpose	Question or Answer
	Means	Content
	Manner	Verification
	Agency	*Form Labels:*
	Reference	Introduction
	Advantage or	Conclusion or
	Disadvantage	Summary
	Association	List
	Relationship	Series
	Possession	Parallel

7. MIMIC THE GREEK DIAGRAM WITH THE ENGLISH TEXT

The English text used in preaching or teaching should be diagrammed to correspond with the Greek diagram. Of course, some tweaking may be needed, depending on how close the English translation follows the word order and phrase structure of the Greek.

The NASB and the ESV, for example, tend to be more word-for-word translations and follow more closely the Greek word order and structure of verb forms (using a "formal equivalence" translation approach). The NIV and the NLT, on the other hand, tend to be more thought-for-thought translations and aim for more effective and dynamic phrasings (using a "functional equivalence" translation approach). Generally speaking, all English translations break up the often long Greek sentences into several shorter ones. Thus, diagramming the Greek first will help the exegete decide which of the sentences in the English text represent subordinate clauses and which represent the author's main clauses. The Greek diagram should control the English diagram and not the vice versa.

The Step 7 example on page 95 above diagrams the NIV text of 1 Peter 1:3–9, directly across from the corresponding (and controlling) Greek diagram on page 94. Note that the same flow of thought is represented in both the Greek and the English layouts.

8. CRAFT A SERMON/LESSON OUTLINE FROM THE DIAGRAM

In exposition, the sermon or lesson outline must come from the text. Thus, the main clauses discovered in the diagramming process drive the main points of the outline. The subordinating phrases and clauses feed the sub-points of the outline. More than one sermon/lesson outline may be developed from a single passage; and sermon/lesson outlines can be more or less detailed depending upon the needs of the intended audience and delivery time allotted.

Step 8 Example

Offered below is a detailed sermon/lesson outline for 1 Peter 1:3-9 that can be truncated as needed. A shorter, less-detailed sermon might cover only the broader points and sub-categories on the left. A longer, more-detailed sermon might cover the sub-points that go deeper to the right.

A Doxology of New Birth—1 Peter 1:3–9

I.   Praise God! He has given us new birth (1 Peter 1:3–5).

   A.   The *standard* by which God gave us this new birth: in his great mercy (1:3a–b).

   B.   The *current result* of our new birth: a living hope (1:3c).

   C.   The *means* of our new birth: through Jesus' resurrection (1:3d).

   D.   The *ultimate result* of our new birth: an inheritance in heaven (1:4). This inheritance is:

      1.   imperishable (v. 4a),

      2.   unspoilable (v. 4b),

      3.   unfading (v. 4c),

      4.   reserved in heaven for you (v. 4d), who are preserved (1:5)

         a.   by God's power (v. 5a),

         b.   through faith (v. 5b),

         c.   for salvation that is coming soon (v. 5c–d).

II. You can rejoice in your new birth despite trials (1 Peter 1:6–9).

   A.   The *time* of suffering: now for a little while (1:6a).

   B.   The *kinds* of suffering: various kinds (1:6b).

   C.   The *reason* for suffering: to refine our extraordinarily precious faith (1:7), which should

      1.   have a genuine quality (v. 7a),

      2.   result in the production of praise (v. 7b),

      3.   and be complete at Jesus Christ's return (v. 7c). After all, Jesus Christ is (1:8–9)

         a.   the object of our "blind" love (v. 8a)

         b.   and, by means of "blind" faith, the source of our joy over our salvation (v. 8b–9).

Sermon/Lesson Overview—1 Peter 1:3–9

The paragraph of 1 Peter 1:3–9 is sometimes referred to as a doxology since it is in praise of God. The first portion of the paragraph describes God, the Father of our Lord Jesus Christ, as the one who provides us with new birth. Peter describes the standard, the means, and two results of this new birth (vv. 3–4a). The ultimate result is an inheritance for believers, an inheritance for which Peter gives a four-part description (v. 4) along with a three-part description of the believer's preservation for that future inheritance (v. 5).

The second portion of the paragraph describes the rejoicing that believers can do regarding the new birth God has provided. This rejoicing can take place despite various temporary sufferings, which serve the purpose of refining our faith. A faith thus refined will be genuine and result in praise when Jesus Christ returns. Indeed, Jesus is the focus of our lives—the object of our love and, by faith, the source of our joy over our salvation.

SPECIAL & PROBLEM ISSUES

A few oddities and the limitations of space can make for some difficulties in phrase diagramming. But these problem areas have several relatively simple solutions, outlined here using examples from 1 Peter 1:3–9.

WORD WRAP-AROUND

This is the layout problem that occurs when a phrase is too long to fit on a single line and the word processor wraps the last part of the phrase to a second line. This phenomenon will happen often enough, especially as the diagram increasingly moves subordinate phrases of other subordinate phrases closer to the right-hand margin. Occasionally, when the line is too long by only a few spaces, this difficulty can be handled by extending the right-hand margin of that one line the necessary few spaces. Many times, however, the word wrap around problem will need a more involved approach.

The simplest approach is to press the return key to force the word wrap at an appropriate place in the phrase and then to tap the space bar to move the wrapped portion all the way over to the right-hand margin (right justified) immediately below the unwrapped portion of the phrase. Then, when drawing the arrow from the subordinate phrase to its ruling clause, the wrapped portion of the phrase will have no arrow coming from it.

This approach, however, can be problematic when the unwrapped portion of the phrase has a word that is modified by a subsequent phrase. An arrow from the subsequent phrase may not be able to point directly to the word it modifies if that word is covered by the wrapped portion of the phrase and the resulting diagram becomes overly complex.

The second approach to handling word wrap-around involves aligning the subordinate phrase under the word it modifies with right justification rather than left justification. Then the arrow is drawn on the right side of the phrase (the norm for diagramming Hebrew) rather than the left (the norm for diagramming Greek). This solution was used in the example passage at 1 Peter 1:7a.

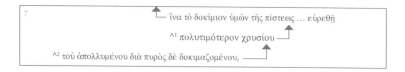

The third approach to handling diagram word wrap-around problems involves three simple steps:

1. Move the wrapping phrase as far left as necessary to keep it all on one line

2. Drop it down one more line space, and then

3. Use the extra line space to draw the arrow back to the right to the word the phrase describes.

Admittedly, this procedure offends the second principle of phrase diagramming: *Subordinate ideas are indented, placed under (or over) the concept to which they are related* (and potentially the third principle: *Parallel ideas are indented the same distance from the left*). Nevertheless, drawing the arrow as described repairs this offense. This method is used above in the example passage at 1 Peter 1:7b.

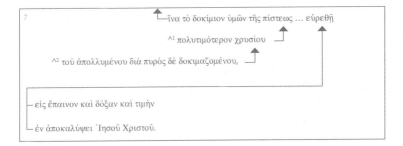

EMBEDDED PHRASES

This problem involves handling a phrase that occurs within another phrase. Since word order in Greek is not as much of an issue as it is in English, embedded phrases occur frequently enough in the Greek New Testament that we must have an approach to diagramming them. As appears to be the case in 1 Peter 1:5 (τοὺς ἐν δυνάμει θεοῦ φρουρουμένους), an embedded phrase can occur in Greek when the phrase functions somewhat like an adjective and takes an attributive position between the noun and its article. There are two ways to deal with embedded phrases.

The first way to deal with embedded phrases maintains the Greek word order but underscores the phrase in order to identify it. This method is simple enough and the underscore itself can be used as the arrow to show which word the phrase modifies. Thus, the example in 1 Peter 1:5 could be drawn like this: τοὺς ἐν δυνάμει θεοῦ φρουρουμένους. A complexity occurs, however, when the embedded phrase modifies a word in a clause other than the one in which it is embedded or a word in the same clause but separated by several other words, maybe even by another embedded phrase. This happens, for example, in 1 Peter 1:8 where ἀγαλλιᾶσθε is separated by δέ from its modifying participial phrase, which has its own descriptive embedded clause (εἰς ὃν ἄρτι μὴ ὁρῶντες πιστεύοντες δὲ ἀγαλλιᾶσθε χαρᾷ ἀνεκλαλήτῳ καὶ δεδοξασμένῃ).

The second way of handling embedded phrases provides for clearer diagrams, but has the disadvantage of disturbing the order of the Greek words. The word order of the original text should be preserved as much as possible so as to protect from wrongly rearranging the text and creating a new message. Where diagramming is made easier by rearranging the phrases and/or words into a smooth order that still represents the same message, ellipses (…) should be used to indicate where a word or phrase was removed and a caret mark (^) should be used to mark that reordered word or phrase (see Guthrie & Duvall, *Biblical Greek Exegesis*, 29). If more than one phrase is reordered and belong to the same ellipses, the caret symbols can be numbered to show their order (^1, ^2, etc.). Examples of this method are seen in the diagram above at 1 Peter 1:3, 5, 7, and 8 (pp. 92 and 94).

It should be noted that embedded phrases in a Greek diagram may not be embedded in the corresponding diagram of the English text. This happens because English translations sometimes reorder the words and phrases to match current speech patterns. This is the case for the example diagram of 1 Peter 1:6–8 in the NIV translation above, as can be seen by comparing it to the Greek diagram (pp. 94-95).

Parallelism and Chiasm

The special literary styles and devices of poetic parallelism and chiasm can lend themselves to some further nuances in diagramming. Indeed, at times an exegete might find it advantageous to draw attention to literary features like chiasm and poetry by diagramming in such a way that highlights those features. But phrase diagramming endeavors to trace the author's flow of thought, so this should always take priority over literary devices in trying to represent the text in a diagram.

Following the third of phrase diagramming's three basic principles (*Parallel ideas are indented the same distance from the left*), parallelisms are naturally diagrammed with the two (or more) parallel lines of text equally indented and connected by the one arrow drawn from them to the word they modify. Poetic parallelisms, however, are parallel both grammatically and conceptually, so some may want to highlight the additional parallelism by making the shaft of the arrow double between the two parallel lines of text.

This same doubled-line method can be used to diagram other constructions like words and phrases in simple apposition, μέν … δέ constructions, or lists where each item in the list serves the same function. So, the example diagram for 1 Peter 1 could be modified to show the apposition in verse 3 and the list in verse 4.

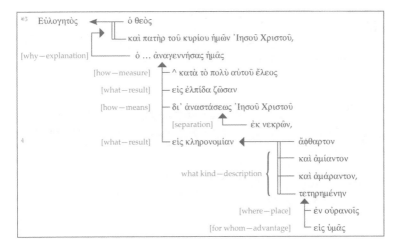

A chiasm occurs when an author reverses a sequence of words or ideas he has just employed. The phrases are said to be ordered ABC:CBA. Other variations sometimes occur (e.g., ABCBA, ABA′B′:B′A′BA, etc.). Some exegetes have found it helpful to layout the phrases of a chiasm using indentation to show the parallel terms. This phenomenon is called "chiasm" because such indenting follows the profile of the Greek letter chi (χ). For example, a chiasm is present in 1 Corinthians 9:19–22:

A: [19] . . . I make myself a slave to everyone, to win as many as possible.

  B: [20] To the Jews I became like a Jew, to win the Jews.

    C: To those under the law I became like one...so as to win those under the law.

    C: [21] To those not having the law I became like one...so as to win those not having the law.

  B: [22] To the weak I became weak, to win the weak.

A: I have become all things to all men so that by all possible means I might save some.

It may be best not to try to incorporate a chiastic drawing within a phrase diagram. On the other hand, rather than using indentation, the key terms of a chiasm could be identified in a phrase diagram by other means such as circling, dashed lines, italics, underlining, different colors, and the like. These same methods can be used to show indirect relationships, antecedents, key terms, and other connections.

DIDACTIC VS. NARRATIVE PASSAGES

Offered below is a phrase diagram of Acts 1:1–5 (in both Greek and English on facing pages). This diagram uses the simpler semantic labels (who, what, when, where, why, which, and how).

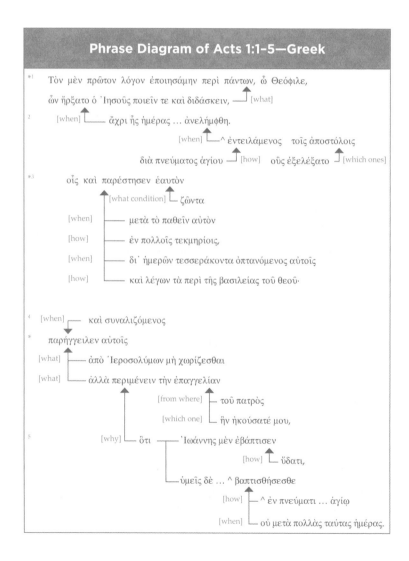

Phrase Diagram of Acts 1:1–5—Greek

*1 Τὸν μὲν πρῶτον λόγον ἐποιησάμην περὶ πάντων, ὦ Θεόφιλε,

ὧν ἤρξατο ὁ Ἰησοῦς ποιεῖν τε καὶ διδάσκειν, ⎯ [what]

2 [when] ⎿ ἄχρι ἧς ἡμέρας … ἀνελήμφθη.

[when] ⎿ ^ ἐντειλάμενος   τοῖς ἀποστόλοις

διὰ πνεύματος ἁγίου ⎯ [how]   οὓς ἐξελέξατο ⎯ [which ones]

*3 οἷς καὶ παρέστησεν ἑαυτὸν

[what condition] ⎿ ζῶντα

[when] ⎯ μετὰ τὸ παθεῖν αὐτὸν

[how] ⎯ ἐν πολλοῖς τεκμηρίοις,

[when] ⎯ δι᾽ ἡμερῶν τεσσεράκοντα ὀπτανόμενος αὐτοῖς

[how] ⎿ καὶ λέγων τὰ περὶ τῆς βασιλείας τοῦ θεοῦ·

4 [when] ⎯ καὶ συναλιζόμενος

* παρήγγειλεν αὐτοῖς

[what] ⎯ ἀπὸ Ἱεροσολύμων μὴ χωρίζεσθαι

[what] ⎿ ἀλλὰ περιμένειν τὴν ἐπαγγελίαν

[from where] ⎯ τοῦ πατρὸς

[which one] ⎿ ἣν ἠκούσατέ μου,

5 [why] ⎿ ὅτι ⎯ Ἰωάννης μὲν ἐβάπτισεν

[how] ⎿ ὕδατι,

⎿ ὑμεῖς δὲ … ^ βαπτισθήσεσθε

[how] ⎯ ^ ἐν πνεύματι … ἁγίῳ

[when] ⎿ οὐ μετὰ πολλὰς ταύτας ἡμέρας.

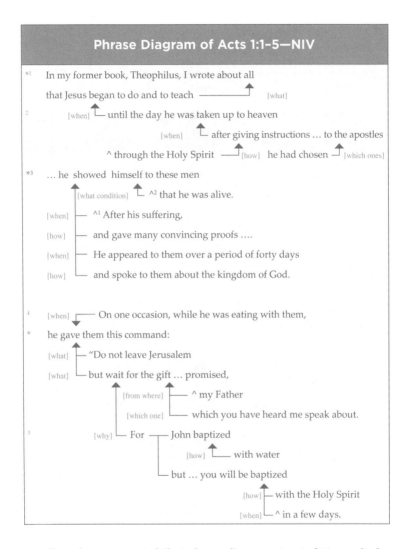

Phrase Diagram of Acts 1:1–5—NIV

*1 In my former book, Theophilus, I wrote about all

that Jesus began to do and to teach ⟶ [what]

2 [when] └ until the day he was taken up to heaven

[when] └ after giving instructions ... to the apostles

^ through the Holy Spirit ⟶ [how] he had chosen ⟶ [which ones]

*3 ... he showed himself to these men

[what condition] └ ^2 that he was alive.

[when] ⊢ ^1 After his suffering,

[how] ⊢ and gave many convincing proofs ....

[when] ⊢ He appeared to them over a period of forty days

[how] └ and spoke to them about the kingdom of God.

4 [when] ⊏ On one occasion, while he was eating with them,

* he gave them this command:

[what] ⊢ "Do not leave Jerusalem

[what] └ but wait for the gift ... promised,

[from where] ⊢ ^ my Father

[which one] └ which you have heard me speak about.

5 [why] └ For ⟶ John baptized

[how] └ with water

└ but ... you will be baptized

[how] ⊢ with the Holy Spirit

[when] └ ^ in a few days.

Some have suggested that phrase diagramming is fitting only for didactic passages, i.e., teaching passages such as those found in the epistles (e.g., Mounce, *A Graded Reader*, xxiii). While certainly didactic passages provide the most colorful arena for phrase diagramming, narrative passages still have a flow of thought for which diagramming may be helpful. Furthermore, narrative books of the NT (the four Gospels and Acts) are composed with interspersed didactic sections in the teachings of Jesus and the sermons of the apostles.

The following sermon/lesson outline is drawn from this phrase diagram of Acts 1:1–5, with its three main points corresponding to the three main points identified in the diagramming process.

Presenting Jesus—Acts 1:1–5

I.   Luke's Former Presentation of Jesus (1:1–2)

    A.   What Jesus began to do and to teach (1:1b)

    B.   Until Jesus' ascension, i.e., the Gospel of Luke (1:2a)

    C.   Where Jesus' followers were introduced and instructed (1:2b)

II. Jesus' Presentation of Himself (1:3)

    A.   Alive (1:3a)

    B.   After his suffering (1:3b)

    C.   In many proofs (1:3c)

    D.   Over a period of forty days (1:3d)

    E.   Instructing his followers about the kingdom of God (1:3e)

III. Commanded Preliminary to Presenting Jesus (1:4–5)

    A.   Instructions while eating: sharing as an everyday event (1:4a)

    B.   Don't go out on your own power (1:4b)

    C.   Go out with the power promised by God the Father: the Holy Spirit (1:4c–5)

Thus, the exercise of phrase diagramming—beginning with the Greek text—can be a relatively quick, easy, and clarifying help to understanding the author's flow of thought, in both didactic and narrative passages. This proves to be a particularly beneficial aid to those desiring to teach and to preach the word of God with sensitivity to its original presentation in the text of the New Testament.

SELECT BIBLIOGRAPHY

GRAMMAR & SYNTAX: Beginning, Intermediate, Advanced.

Black, David Alan. *Learn to Read New Testament Greek*. Expanded ed. Nashville: Broadman & Holman, 1994. (*B*)

Black, David Alan. *It's Still Greek to Me: An Easy-to-Understand Guide to Intermediate Greek*. Grand Rapids: Baker, 1998. (*I*)

Blass, Friedrich, and Albert Debrunner. *A Greek Grammar of the New Testament and Other Early Christian Literature*. Trans. and rev. Robert W. Funk. Chicago: University of Chicago, 1961. (*A*)

Brooks, James A., and Carlton L. Winbery. *Syntax of New Testament Greek*. Lanham, MD: University Press of America, 1979. (*I*)

Burton, Earnest de Witt. *Syntax of the Moods and Tenses in New Testament Greek*. 2nd ed. Edinburgh: T. & T. Clark, 1894. (*A*)

Campbell, Constantine R. *Basics of Verbal Aspect in Biblical Greek*. Grand Rapids: Zondervan, 2008. (*I*)

Dobson, John H. *Learn New Testament Greek*. 3rd ed. Carlisle: Piquant, 2005; Grand Rapids: Baker, 2005. (*B*)

Duff, Jeremy. *The Elements of New Testament Greek*. 3rd ed. Cambridge: Cambridge University Press, 2005. (*B*)

Fanning, Buist M. *Verbal Aspect in New Testament Greek*. Oxford: Clarendon Press, 1990. (*A*)

Goodwin, William Watson. *Syntax of the Moods and Tenses of the Greek Verb*. Rev. ed. London: Macmillan, 1889. (*A*)

Greenlee, J. Harold. *A Concise Exegetical Grammar of New Testament Greek*. 5th ed. Grand Rapids: Eerdmans, 1986. (*B*)

Hewett, James Allen. *New Testament Greek: A Beginning and Intermediate Grammar*. Peabody, MA: Hendrickson, 1986. (*I*)

Lamerson, Samuel. *English Grammar to Ace New Testament Greek*. Grand Rapids: Zondervan, 2004. (*B*)

Long, Gary A. *Grammatical Concepts 101 for Biblical Greek: Learning Biblical Greek Grammatical Concepts Through English Grammar*. Peabody, MA: Hendrickson, 2006. (*B*)

McKay, K. L. *A New Syntax of the Verb in New Testament Greek: An Aspectual Approach*. Studies in Biblical Greek 3. New York: Peter Lang, 1994. (*I*)

Moulton, James Hope, W. F. Howard, and Nigel Turner. *A Grammar of New Testament Greek*. 4 vols. [Vol. 1, *Prolegomena* (Moulton); vol. 2, *Accidence and Word-Formation* (Howard); vol. 3, *Syntax* (Turner); vol. 4—*Style* (Turner).] Edinburgh: T. & T. Clark, 1908–76. (*A*)

Mounce, William D. *Basics of Biblical Greek Grammar*. 3rd ed. Grand Rapids: Zondervan, 2009. (*B*)

Mounce, William D. *Biblical Greek: A Compact Guide*. Grand Rapids: Zondervan, 2011. (*B*)

Mounce, William D. *Biblical Greek Laminated Sheet*. Zondervan Get an A! Study Guides. Grand Rapids: Zondervan, 2005. (*B*)

Mueller, Walter. *Grammatical Aids for Students of New Testament Greek*. Grand Rapids: Eerdmans, 1972. (*I*)

Porter, Stanley E. *Idioms of the Greek New Testament*. 2nd ed. Biblical Languages: Greek 2. Sheffield: Sheffield Academic Press, 1996. (*I*)

Porter, Stanely E. *Verbal Aspect in the Greek of the New Testament, with Reference to Tense and Mood*. Studies in Biblical Greek, 1. New York: Peter Lang, 1993. (*A*)

Porter, Stanley E., Jeffrey T. Reed, and Matthew Brook O'Donnell. *Fundamentals of New Testament Greek*. Grand Rapids: Eerdmans, 2010. (*B*)

Robertson, A. T. *A Grammar of the Greek New Testament in the Light of Historical Research*, 4th ed. Nashville: Broadman, 1934. (*A*)

Robinson, Thomas A. *Mastering New Testament Greek: Essential Tools for Students*. Peabody, MA: Hendrickson, 2007. (*B*)

Wallace, Daniel B. *The Basics of New Testament Syntax: An Intermediate Greek Grammar (The Abridgment of Greek Grammar Beyond the Basics: An Exegetical Syntax of the New Testament)*. Grand Rapids: Zondervan, 2000. (*I*)

Wallace, Daniel B. *Greek Grammar Beyond the Basics: An Exegetical Syntax of the New Testament*. Grand Rapids: Zondervan, 1997. (*A*)

Wallace, Daniel B. *New Testament Greek Syntax Laminated Sheet*. Zondervan Get an A! Study Guides. Grand Rapids: Zondervan, 2009. (*I*)

Young, Norman H. *Syntax Lists for Students of New Testament Greek*. Cambridge: Cambridge University Press, 2001. (*I*)

Young, Richard A. *Intermediate New Testament Greek: A Linguistic and Exegetical Approach*. Nashville: Broadman & Holman, 1994. (*I*)

Zerwick, Maximilian. *Biblical Greek Illustrated by Examples*. Trans., Joseph Smith. SPIB 114. Rome: Pontifical Biblical Institute, 1963. (*A*)

NEW TESTAMENT IN GREEK: Standard Critical NT Texts.

Aland, Kurt, et al., eds. *The Greek New Testament*. 4th rev. ed. New York: American Bible Society, 2001. [UBS⁴]

Hodges, Zane C., and Arthur L. Farstad, eds. *The Greek New Testament According to the Majority Text with Apparatus*. 2nd ed. Nashville: Nelson, 1985. [Majority]

Holmes, Michael W., ed. *The Greek New Testament: SBL Edition*. Atlanta, GA: Society of Biblical Literature, 2010; Bellingham, WA: Logos Bible Software, 2010. See http://sblgnt.com. [SBLGNT]

Nestle, Erwin, and Kurt Aland, et al., eds. *Novum Testamentum Graece*. 28th rev. ed. Stuttgart: German Bible Society, 2012. [NA²⁸]

Robinson, Maurice A. , and William G. Pierport, eds. *New Testament in the Original Greek: Byzantine Textform 2005*. Southborough, MA: Chilton, 2005. [Byz]

GREEK READERS: For Verse-by-Verse NT Greek NT Helps.

Burer, Michael H., and Jeffrey E. Miller. *A New Reader's Lexicon of the Greek New Testament*. Grand Rapids: Kregel, 2008.

Friberg, Timothy, and Barbara Friberg, eds. *Analytical Greek New Testament: Greek Text Analysis*. Baker's Greek New Testament Library, 1. Grand Rapids: Baker, 1981.

Goodrich, Richard J., and Albert L. Lukaszewski. *A Reader's Greek New Testament*. Grand Rapids: Zondervan, 2003.

Kubo, Sakae. *A Reader's Greek-English Lexicon of the New Testament and A Beginner's Guide for the Translation of New Testament Greek*. Andrews University Monographs 4. Grand Rapids: Zondervan, 1975.

Perschbacher, Wesley J. *Refresh Your Greek: Practical Helps for Reading the New Testament*. Chicago: Moody Press, 1989.

Rogers, Cleon L., Jr., and Cleon L. Rogers III. *The New Linguistic and Exegetical Key to the Greek New Testament*. Grand Rapids: Zondervan, 1998.

Zerwick, Max, and Mary Grosvenor. *A Grammatical Analysis of the Greek New Testament*. Unabridged, 5th rev. ed. Rome: Pontifical Biblical Institute, 1996.

GREEK-ENGLISH INTERLINEARS: For Parallel Reading.

Kohlenberger, John R., III, ed. *The Greek New Testament: UBS4 With NRSV & NIV*. Grand Rapids: Zondervan, 1993. [UBS[4]]

Majority Text Greek New Testament Interlinear. Nashville: Nelson, 2007. [Majority]

Marshall, Alfred, ed. *The NASB Interlinear Greek-English New Testament: The Nestle Greek Text with a Literal English Translation*. Grand Rapids: Zondervan, 1984. [NA[27]]

Nestle, Erwin, and Kurt Aland, et al., eds. *Greek-English New Testament: Nestle-Aland 28th Edition and English Standard Version*. Wheaton: Crossway, 2012. [NA[28]]

CONCORDANCES, LEXICONS, LISTS: For Word Studies.

Balz, Horst, and Gerhard Schneider, eds. *Exegetical Dictionary of the New Testament*. 3 vols. Grand Rapids: Eerdmans, 1978–80.

Bauer, Walter. *A Greek-English Lexicon of the New Testament and Other Early Christian Literature*. Trans., W. F. Arndt and F. W. Gingrich; 2nd ed. Augmented, F. W. Gingrich and F. W. Danker. Chicago: University of Chicago, 1979.

Brown, Colin, ed. *The New International Dictionary of the New Testament*. 3 vols. Grand Rapids: Zondervan, 1975–78.

Concordance to the Novum Testamentum Graece/Koncordanz zum Novum Testamentum Graece. Ed. the Institute for New Testament Textual Research and the Computer Center of Munster University with the collaboration of H. Bachmann and W. A. Slaby. 3rd ed. New York: De Gruyter, 1987.

Danker, Frederick William, rev. ed. *A Greek-English Lexicon of the New Testament and Other Early Christian Literature*. 3rd ed. Based on Walter Bauer's *Griechisch-deutsches Wörterbuch zu den Schriften des Neuen Testaments und der frühchristlichen Literatur*, 6th ed., ed. Kurt Aland and Barbara Aland, with Viktor Reichmann and on previous English editions by W. F. Arndt, F. W. Gingrich, and F. W. Danker. Chicago: University of Chicago Press, 2000.

Harris, Murray J. *Prepositions and Theology in the Greek New Testament*. Grand Rapids: Zondervan, 2012.

Kittel, Gerhard, and G. Friedrich, eds. *Theological Dictionary of the New Testament*. 10 vols. Trans. Geoffrey W. Bromiley. Grand Rapids: Eerdmans, 1964–74.

Liddell, Henry George, and Robert Scott. *A Greek-English Lexicon*. New ed., H. S. Jones, et al. Oxford: Clarendon, 1940 + Barber, E. A. et al. *Supplement*. 1968.

Louw, Johannes P., and Eugene A. Nida, eds. *Greek-English Lexicon of the New Testament Based on Semantic Domains*. 2nd ed. 2 vols. New York: United Bible Societies, 1989.

Mounce, William D. *The Analytical Lexicon to the Greek New Testament*. Zondervan Greek Reference Series. Grand Rapids: Zondervan, 1993.

Mounce, William D., gen. ed. *Mounce's Complete Expository Dictionary of Old & New Testament Words*. Grand Rapids: Zondervan, 2006.

Trenchard, Warren C. *Complete Vocabulary Guide to the Greek New Testament*. Rev. ed. Grand Rapids: Zondervan, 1998.

Trenchard, Warren C. *A Concise Dictionary of New Testament Greek*. Cambridge: Cambridge University Press, 2003.

Wilson, Mark, and Jason Oden. *Mastering New Testament Greek Vocabulary Through Semantic Domains*. Grand Rapids: Kregel, 2003.

DIAGRAMMING: For More on Visual Representation.

Brooks, James A., and Carlton L. Winbery. *Syntax of New Testament Greek*. Lanham, MD: University Press, 1979. Pp. 154–86.

Cotterell, Peter, and Max Turner. *Linguistics & Biblical Interpretation*. Downers Grove: InterVarsity Press, 1989. Pp. 188–229.

Easley, Kendell H. *User-Friendly Greek: A Common Sense Approach to the Greek New Testament*. Nashville: Broadman & Holman, 1994. Pp. 19–34.

Fee, Gordon D. *New Testament Exegesis: A Handbook for Students and Pastors*. 3rd ed. Louisville: Westminster/John Knox, 2002. Pp. 41–58.

Guthrie, George H., and J. Scott Duvall. *Biblical Greek Exegesis: A Graded Approach to Learning Intermediate and Advanced Greek*. Grand Rapids: Zondervan, 1998. Pp. 23–53.

Kantenwein, Lee L. *Diagrammatical Analysis*. Rev. ed. Winona Lake, IN: BMH Books, 1985.

Kaiser, Walter C. *Toward an Exegetical Theology: Biblical Exegesis for Preaching and Teaching*. Grand Rapids: Baker, 1981. Pp. 99–103, 165–81.

LaSor, William Sanford. *Handbook of New Testament Greek: An Inductive Approach Based on the Greek Text of Acts*. 2 vols. Grand Rapids, Eerdmans, 1973. 2:137–44.

MacDonald, William G. *Greek Enchiridion: A Concise Handbook of Grammar for Translation and Exegesis*. Peabody, MA: Hendrickson, 1989. Pp. 139–52.

McKnight, Scot. "New Testament Greek Grammatical Analysis." In *Introducing New Testament Interpretation*, ed. Scot McKnight, Guides to New Testament Exegesis. Grand Rapids: Baker, 1996. Pp. 89–95.

Mounce, William D. *A Graded Reader of Biblical Greek*. Grand Rapids: Zondervan, 1996. Pp. xv–xxiii.

Mounce, William D. *Greek for the Rest of Us: Using Greek Tools Without Mastering Biblical Greek*. Grand Rapids: Zondervan, 2003. Pp. 55–77, 109–41.

Osborne, Grant R. *The Hermeneutical Spiral: A Comprehensive Introduction to Biblical Interpretation*. 2nd ed. Downers Grove: InterVarsity Press, 2006. Pp. 45–51.

Shreiner, Thomas R. *Interpreting the Pauline Epistles*. 2nd ed. Guides to New Testament Exegesis. Grand Rapids: Baker, 2011. Pp. 69–124.

Smith, Jay E. "Sentence Diagramming, Clausal Layouts, and Exegetical Outlining: Tracing the Argument." Pp 73–134 in *Interpreting the New Testament Text: Introduction to the Art and Science of Exegesis*, ed. Darrell L. Bock and Buist M. Fanning. Wheaton: Crossway, 2006.

ELECTRONIC RESOURCES: Software & Internet Greek Aids.

Accordance Bible Software. Altamonte Springs, FL: OakTree Software. (This is GRAMCORD for Macintosh users, now also operable in Windows environments). See http://www.accordancebible.com.

Berding, Kenneth. *Sing and Learn New Testament Greek: The Easiest Way to Learn Greek Grammar*. Grand Rapids: Zondervan, 2008 (audio CD).

Bible Research by Michael Marlowe. (A collection of links to internet resources for students to Scripture). See http://www.bible-researcher.com.

Bible Web App. See http://biblewebapp.com.

Biblearc. Minneapolis, MN: Bethlehem College and Seminary. See http://www.biblearc.com.

BibleWorks. Norfolk, VA: BibleWorks, LLC. See http://www.bibleworks.com.

Biblos.com. Glassport, PA: Online Parallel Bible Project. See http://biblos.com.

Duff, Jeremy, and Jonathan T. Pennington. *New Testament Greek Listening Materials: For the Elements of New Testament Greek, 3rd Edition*. Cambridge: Cambridge University Press, 2005 (audio CD). See also http:www.nt-greek.net.

GRAMCORD. Battle Ground, WA: The GRAMCORD Institute. (A grammatical concordance tool for searching the Greek New Testament). See http://www.gramcord.org.

Hoffeditz, David M., and J. Michael Thigpen. *iVocab Biblical Greek*. Grand Rapids: Kregel, 2007 (audio-visual flashcard software for MP3 players, cellular phones, and computers).

Logos Bible Software. Bellingham, WA: Logos Research Systems, Inc. See http://www.logos.com/scholars.

Mounce, William D. *Basics of Biblical Greek Vocabulary Audio*. Grand Rapids: Zondervan, 2006 (audio CD). See also http://www.Teknia.com.

New Testament Gateway by Mark Goodacre. (A collection of links to internet resources for New Testament research). See http://www.ntgateway.com.

PC Study Bible. Seattle, WA: Biblesoft, Inc. See http://www.biblesoft.com

Pennington, Jonathan T. *Readings in the Greek New Testament*. Grand Rapids: Zondervan, 2004 (audio CDs or audio download).

Pennington, Jonathan T. *New Testament Greek Vocabulary: Learn on the Go*. Grand Rapids: Zondervan, 2001 (audio CDs or audio download).

QuickVerse and WORDsearch Bible Software. Austin, TX: WORDsearch Corp., LLC. See https://www.wordsearchbible.com.

Thesaurus Linguae Graecae. (A research center at the University of California—Irvine is creating a comprehensive digital library of Greek literature from antiquity to the present. Most Greek literary texts from Homer to AD 1453 are already available). See http://www.tlg.uci.edu.

The Unbound Bible. (A Website sponsored by Biola University with multiple Bible study resources including biblical language lexicons and a Greek parsing tool). See http://unbound.biola.edu.

NT COMMENTARIES: Using Greek to Comment in English.

The Exegetical Guide to the Greek New Testament (EGGNT; ed. Murray J. Harris; published by B & H [formerly by Eerdmans]). This projected 20-volume series moves from grammatical analysis to exegesis to sermon outline.

The New International Greek Testament Commentary (NIGTC; ed. I. Howard Marshall and Donald A. Hagner; published by Eerdmans/Paternoster). This series is aimed at students of Greek seeking a theological understanding of the text.

The Zondervan Exegetical Commentary on the New Testament (ZECNT; ed. Clinton E. Arnold; published by Zondervan). The volumes in this series offer phrase diagramming, an exegetical outline, explanation, and theological application for each passage.